Story Machines

Mike Sharples is Emeritus Professor of Educational Technology at The Open University, UK. He is the author of *How We Write: Writing as Creative Design*. His other works include *Computers and Thought: A Practical Introduction to Artificial Intelligence* and over 300 books and papers on artificial intelligence, computers and writing and educational technology.

Rafael Pérez y Pérez is a full Professor at Universidad Autónoma Metropolitana at Cuajimalpa, México City. He specializes in computational creativity, particularly models for narrative generation, and has led the Association for Computational Creativity. His works include *MEXICA: 20 Years – 20 Stories*, *Creatividad Computacional* and diverse papers on artificial intelligence and computational creativity. His website is www.rafaelperezyperez.com.

D1615038

Story Machines

How Computers Have Become Creative Writers

MIKE SHARPLES AND RAFAEL PÉREZ Y PÉREZ

Routledge
Taylor & Francis Group

LONDON AND NEW YORK

Cover image: © Getty Images

First published 2022
by Routledge
4 Park Square, Milton Park, Abingdon, Oxon OX14 4RN

and by Routledge
605 Third Avenue, New York, NY 10158

Routledge is an imprint of the Taylor & Francis Group, an informa business

British Library Cataloguing-in-Publication Data
A catalogue record for this book is available from the British Library

Library of Congress Cataloging-in-Publication Data
A catalog record has been requested for this book

ISBN: 978-0-367-75195-1 (hbk)
ISBN: 978-0-367-75197-5 (pbk)
ISBN: 978-1-003-16143-1 (ebk)

DOI: 10.4324/9781003161431

Typeset in Dante and Avenir
by Apex CoVantage, LLC

Printed and bound in Great Britain by
TJ Books Limited, Padstow, Cornwall

To Minji and Olive, constant companions

To Yani and Susana, two superstars in my life

Contents

Epigraph   ix

Preface   xi

1 Can a computer write a story?   1

2 Human story machines   14

3 Artificial versifying   26

4 Automatic novel writers   45

5 The shape of a story   58

6 The program that swallowed the internet   70

7 Storyworlds   83

8 Being creative   101

9 Modelling the mind of a writer   115

10 Build your own story generator   126

11 Capacity for empathy   141

   Acknowledgements   152

   Notes   153

   Further reading   173

   Index   175

Transcribe each Line composed by this Machine,
Record the fleeting Thoughts as they arise:
A Line, once lost, may ne-er again be seen;
A Thought, once flown, perhaps for ever flies.

Part of an inscription on the front panel of Eureka, a 19th century machine to generate Latin verse.

Preface

We have all read stories that have been written by software. They are just not labelled as such. Perhaps the most well-known are the choose-your-own-adventure books where readers are given a series of choices and are instructed to turn to a certain page for the next chapter. For the most part, the stories are successful because they are written in a way that allows each person to feel as if they are the protagonist who is making the decisions. But these are just the beginnings of what's to come. Imagine what would happen if the machines that create these stories also became able to write original content. What would that mean for the way in which the stories are conceived, the way in which they are written, and the way in which they are read?

We didn't compose that first paragraph – a computer did. We instructed it to "Write the opening paragraph for a book about the effect on people and society of computers that generate stories", then copied and pasted the result (it generated five versions and we chose the best).[1] We could have asked the same program to write a short piece of fiction, a blog, a poem, or a tweet. It can also answer trivia questions and translate languages. You might query its assertion that "we have all read stories that have been written by software", but as an opening paragraph, it sounds plausible.

Computers can now write original short stories, stories that can entertain and persuade others. What they can't do is reflect on what they have written. Artificial intelligence (AI) has reached that dangerous point where computers can generate convincing text, but the software lacks common sense and moral purpose. Other researchers in AI and creativity have taken a different approach, to design programs that are less fluent in language but can interpret and revise what they have composed. If these two types of programs can be combined, it may be possible to build a universal story machine. What then?

In this book we explore story machines, past, present and future. For over a thousand years, human writers have been fascinated by the possibility of machines that can sing, dance and tell stories. Everyone can relate to the human act of storytelling, yet authors through the ages have portrayed their craft as a mysterious creative process – inspired by dreams, motivated by primal urges, transforming lived experience into prose. What will be the influence on writers and society of computer programs that tell believable stories? Should we celebrate the rise of a new creative being? What can we learn about human creativity from seeing how they work? Will story machines replace writers or assist them?

In 1987, Margaret Boden founded the School of Cognitive and Computing Sciences (COGS) at the University of Sussex in the UK.[2] She brought together psychologists, mathematicians, philosophers, linguists and computer scientists in one building to explore the nature of thinking in humans and machines. COGS was formed just as AI was going through one of its periodic rises, with renewed interest in robotics and neural networks.

The reason why Boden, humanist and philosopher, set up COGS was not to train students for careers in AI but to understand what it means to be human.[3] By building computer models of minds, we can explore fundamental questions like "What is intelligence?", "How do humans understand language?" and "How can we become more creative?". When an AI program performs an intellectual task like translating language or diagnosing disease, it indicates a possible mechanism for human cognition that can be explored in more detail. Where AI fails – such as in performing feats of logic but not being able to think and act like a child – it reveals the power of the human mind to learn and adapt.

Each Wednesday afternoon the school would gather for a Work in Progress Seminar, where young researchers, some later to become distinguished professors, would argue with passion about artificial minds and autonomous robots. Undergraduates arriving at the school to study psychology or philosophy took a compulsory course in Computers and Thought where they wrote programs to simulate psychotherapists and discussed creativity in humans and machines.

In those days, as a junior academic at COGS, I (Mike) found my niche by studying how people write. I gained funding to design a writer's assistant and formed a research group on cognition and creative writing. What started as a project to help children develop their writing abilities became a fascination with how authors work – their habits, mental processes, strategies and tools – which I later turned into a book on *How We Write: Writing as Creative Design*.[4] I gathered together a rich assortment of researchers and graduate students, some of whom designed programs for story generation.

In 1993, I gave a talk at what is now called the British Science Festival about our work at Sussex on programs to tell stories. At the end of the talk I was ushered into a room filled with journalists who fired questions such as "When will a computer write a novel?" and "Are you putting us out of a job?". Flustered at the unexpected interest in our research, I jabbered about computers not being able to portray the narrator's experience or push back the boundaries of language. Pressed into giving a date when a computer would write a novel, I said maybe in ten or 20 years (that sounded sufficiently far in the future that it wouldn't come back to haunt me).

The next day, national newspapers ran articles about how researchers at Sussex University "had their sights set on a Mills and Boon romance novel and a James Bond thriller". According to *The Daily Telegraph* newspaper, I had said, "How can a machine describe Bond's snobbery, the flavour of a wine, the pattern of sunlight through leaves, or the feeling of loneliness, since it knows nothing about these things. . . . But the fundamental structure of a Bond plot is much easier to program. They are all very similar, following classic fairy tales where M is the King, Bond is the Knight, the villain is the dragon and there is a Maiden who must be rescued. . . . I believe that in 10 to 20 years' time it will be possible for a machine to write a novel and for no one to know that it has not been written by a human."[5]

That was then. It is now 30 years since I gave the talk. Has a computer written a novel? Could it describe the feeling of loneliness or even follow the structure of a James Bond plot? We'll address these questions in this book.

I (Rafael) arrived at COGS to study in a Master's programme in AI. I was very happy to work in a multidisciplinary context, because I had previously always studied in traditional disciplinary environments. One day I got an email from an academic in COGS named Mike Sharples inviting me to develop my Master's dissertation in topics related to creativity. That is how I discovered the field of computational creativity. I got so excited with the possibility of blending my programming skills with my fascination for mental processes in humans, particularly those related to creativity, that I decided to study for a DPhil and asked Mike to be my tutor. That was best academic decision ever, one that today still keeps on producing exciting results (like this book).

In 1996 I started developing a computer model for narrative generation called MEXICA, based on Mike's Engagement-Reflection account of creative writing. By December 1997, for the defence of my thesis, I had a fully running version of MEXICA. Since then, I have enriched the program to evaluate its own stories, generate texts in English and Spanish, and work with other systems to produce collaborative narratives. In 2019, a book of 20 short stories authored by MEXICA was published.[6] This book has been presented at Guadalajara's International Book Fair and other venues. I have also been Chair for almost five years of the Association for Computational Creativity.[7]

Together, we explore the fascinating worlds of computer storytelling. We show how language is itself a machine to generate meaningful prose and poetry. We uncover early poetry generators, track the development of increasingly sophisticated attempts to replicate human creativity in computer programs, and demonstrate tellable tales composed by AI.

Each new development indicates how human creative writing can be replicated by machines, yet it also reveals the power of the lived experience. Each attempt to produce believable stories shows what is missing from computer simulations: that telling stories about our lives is what makes us uniquely human. Are you sitting comfortably? Then we'll begin.

Can a computer write a story?

1

Can a computer write a story?

Yes, it's easy. You just type a short story into a word processor, press the print button, and out it comes. The French publisher Short Édition has installed story vending machines in cities and universities around the world to promote the reading of literature.[1] At the touch of a button, the machine prints a short story for free on eco-friendly paper the width of a toilet roll. There's no cost to use the machine and readers can choose from stories that take one minute, three minutes, or five minutes to read. The vending machines have dispensed more than 35 million short stories written by 10,000 independent authors.

It's a great idea, but these stories are written by humans, not computers. Could a computer create new, original stories?

Well, you could chop already-written stories into smaller pieces – single events, dialogues, descriptions – then code a computer program to select some at random and string them together, slotting in consistent characters throughout. Here's an example we prepared by hand:

> I had called upon my friend, Mr Quentin Hall, one day in the autumn
> of last year and found him deep in conversation with a very stout
> florid-faced elderly gentleman, with fiery red hair. My friend rose

DOI: 10.4324/9781003161431-1

lazily from his arm-chair and stood with his hands in the pockets of his dressing gown. I was surprised. I looked at the clock. Both Hall and I had a weakness for the Turkish Bath. As Hall turned up the lamp a light fell upon a card on the table. In his right hand he had a slip of litmus paper. Then he stood before the fire, and looked me over in his singular introspective fashion.

"You have a case, Hall?", I remarked.

"Very sorry to knock you up, Wilberforce," said he, "but it's the common lot this morning."

"My dear fellow, I wouldn't miss it for anything."

We constructed this opening for a short story by choosing, at random, one opening sentence from the collection of Sherlock Holmes short stories, followed by random sentences from the first paragraphs of other stories in the collection, then some random pieces of opening dialogue, with the names of characters altered. Although the names of the characters have been changed and the passage makes little overall sense, the style is still clearly that of Sir Arthur Conan Doyle.

The sense of harmony that comes from writing in an identifiable style was one of the ploys used in Sheldon Klein's Automatic Novel Writer program created in the 1970s.[2] Klein claimed that his program could produce 2,100-word murder mystery stories in less than 20 seconds. Here are the first 80 or so words from one of its offerings.[3]

```
Wonderful smart Lady Buxley was rich. Ugly oversexed
Lady Buxley was single. John was Lady Buxley's nephew.
Impoverished irritable John was evil. Handsome oversexed
John Buxley was single. John hated Edward. John Buxley
hated Dr. Bartholomew Hume. Brilliant Hume was evil.
Hume was oversexed. Handsome Dr. Bartholomew was single.
Kind easygoing Edward was rich. Oversexed Lord Edward
was ugly. Lord Edward was married to Lady Jane. Edward
liked Lady Jane. Edward was not jealous. Lord Edward
disliked John. Pretty jealous Jane liked Lord Edward.
```

The program followed the flow of a stereotypical mystery story, introducing some characters at an English country manor, then progressing though a flirtation between two characters, love making, threats, and a murder. For each scene it chose from a stock of pre-prepared sentences, giving consistent names for the characters. The Automatic Novel Writer undoubt-edly produced prose in the style of murder mysteries, but the stories it told were rambling and tedious. The extract certainly doesn't entice you to read the remaining 2,000 words of the story.

That's not surprising. Authors don't just pluck out phrases at random. They form them into a logical order to make an interesting and coherent plot

Klein's program had a notion of plot, in its "murder flow-chart", but it was very rigid. Its language was stilted and repetitive. What's needed is a way to describe the structure of a whole set of plots that can then be used as a source for varied story structures.

The diagram on the next page shows a plot generator for science fiction stories. It was first published in 1971 in *National Lampoon*,[4] an American humour magazine and a somewhat unlikely place for an article on automated creativity. By following the arrows from the top to the bottom of the diagram you can produce variations on a sci-fi theme. Here's one of many:

> Earth scientists discover giant reptiles which are friendly but mis-understood and are radioactive and cannot be killed by the Army, Navy, Marine Corps and / or coastguard so scientists invent a weapon which fails but they die from catching chicken pox (The End).

The Science Fiction Horror Movie Pocket Computer, as *National Lampoon* called it, might be a source of ideas to an aspiring author or movie maker, but a far greater challenge is to devise some small set of rules that could describe or generate the complete works of a classic storyteller such as Aesop or the brothers Grimm. Nearly one hundred years ago the Russian folklorist and scholar Vladimir Propp did just that. He analyzed a hun-dred Russian folktales and discovered that not only did they have recurring acts, such as "acquisition of a magical object", but that characters in an act could be replaced by others without damaging the structure of the tale.[5] So, for example, the act of "a witch steals the King's favourite horse" could be changed to "a dragon (or ogre, or rival King) steals the King's ring (or princess, or healing potion)" and the tale would still have a solid structure.

Propp produced a masterly analysis of folk tales and founded the study of literary structures, but he didn't have the means to turn his analyses around and create new story structures. It took a further forty years to bring together the essential ingredients: a way to describe the structure of stories by means

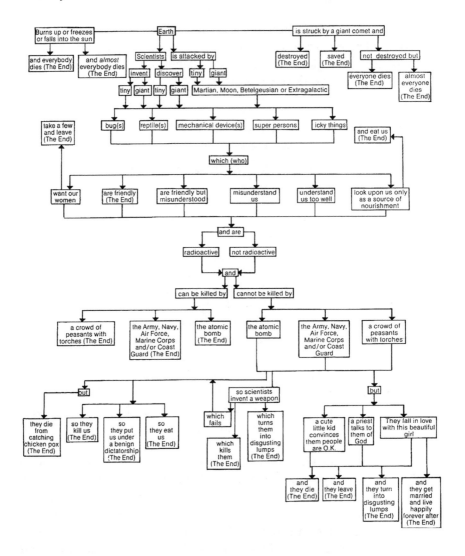

of formal rules (called a story grammar), plus a method to automatically follow those rules to generate new story outlines.[6] Code that in a computer program and it can output thousands of different outline stories.

Here's the first rule of a grammar to generate the outline of a typical story:

STORY – > INTRODUCTION + ACTION* + CONCLUSION

The rule says: "A story consists of an Introduction, followed by one or more Actions, followed by a Conclusion". The asterisk after ACTION means it can be repeated multiple times. This makes intuitive sense. Most stories start with an introduction to set the scene, then have many pieces of action, and then round off with a conclusion. Each of these elements is broken down into further elements such as ACTION_SEQUENCE and COMPLICATION. By following the rules in a systematic way you or a computer can generate endless story outlines.

If you pay a large sum of money for a course on How to Write a Great Novel, you'll probably get, along with much good advice from professional writers, some variant of a story grammar as a way to come up with outlines for your novel. We'll return to story grammars later in the book.

But not all stories fit into the same structure, and what about the characters?

We can produce a story grammar that covers a wide range of story types, from medieval French epics to detective stories. It is based on the insight that such stories have similar structures that move from a lack of or a need for something (in a detective story it is usually the lack of a suspect) to a situation where the lack is either resolved or repeated.

Story grammars only cover the outline of a story. We need a further method to flesh this out with interesting and believable characters. TAILOR is a computer program that generates stories in the style of Aesop's fables.[7] It is based on the principle that stories arise from a character's lack or need, but instead of following a story grammar it sets up a need for one of the characters, places the character in a location, and gives it a plan to satisfy that need. For example, the need to find warmth would cause the character to travel in search of a fire. To complicate matters and provide some interest in the story, the program introduces other characters who try to impede the plan by concealing objects or offering misleading advice. In effect, the program winds up the clockwork of a needy character, puts the character into a fictitious world, and records what happens. Here's an example from TAILOR of a story about an arctic tern named Truman who sets off on a quest to build a home but is thwarted by Horace, the devious polar bear:

> Once upon a time there was an arctictern named Truman. Truman was homeless. Truman needed a nest. He flew to the shore. Truman looked for some twigs. Truman found no twigs. He flew to the tundra. He met a polarbear named Horace. Truman asked Horace where there were some twigs. Horace concealed the twigs. Horace told Truman

```
there were some twigs on the iceberg. Truman flew to
the iceberg. He found no twigs. Horace walked to the
shore. He swam to the iceberg. Horace looked for some
meat. He found some meat. He ate Truman. Truman died.
```

This is a story that makes some sense. There's a main character, Truman the tern, with a believable goal, building a nest. Truman carries out actions that match his character and the setting. But the task is complicated by an adversary, Horace, who hides the twigs. Horace also has a need, for meat. He tells Truman there are twigs on the iceberg and, in a final showdown, confronts the hapless bird and eats him. It's a good basis for a somewhat gruesome tale.

Impressive! How many lousy stories did TAILOR have to generate before it came up with that good one?

TAILOR had no means to distinguish an interesting story from a tedious one. That had to be done by the program's creators, so naturally they only presented the best ones. They didn't say how many bad stories they rejected to find one good one. This raises the issue of tellability.

A tellable story should not merely be interesting, but it should give the reader some reward for having finished it: an insight into the human condition, a moral, or just a final twist to the plot. The story about Truman and Horace is, arguably, tellable. It has a neat twist at the end where Horace satisfies his need for food by eating the main character.

But the program doesn't know that. The TAILOR program has no way of evaluating its own tales. It just generates story after story, some interesting, some pointless, with no insight into how they will be received by the reader. TALE-SPIN is an earlier program based on similar principles to TAILOR, and here is an example of a pointless story it generated:[8]

```
Once upon a time there was a dishonest fox and a vain
crow. One day the crow was sitting in his tree holding
a piece of cheese. He became hungry and swallowed the
cheese. The fox walked over to the crow. The end.
```

The story may have some curiosity value, but it's not tellable. It doesn't capture the reader's imagination. It starts well by introducing two characters and their traits, then sets the scene by describing the crow holding a piece of cheese in his tree. Then, instead introducing the second character to build tension (perhaps to steal the cheese or to offer better food), the story generator just resolves the crow's need by having him eat the cheese. The cunning fox arrives too late!

It may be possible to add an extra module to a story generating program to evaluate each finished story and reject those that do not pass its quality threshold. Many word processors such as Microsoft Word have modules to check a document's readability, but these can only assess the surface properties of the text, such as the length of its sentences and the average number of syllables per word.[9] A score for "interestingness" or "tellability" requires a program that delves deep into the meaning of a story.

However, the difficulty of getting a program to interpret its own output could be avoided if the system has built-in "tellability", so that it produces only tellable stories. Scott Turner's MINSTREL program generates short stories of what he called "King Arthur and his knights" type.[10] The program stores a set of templates, each with a well-known moral such as "pride goes before a fall". It then fills in the details from a stock of interesting story fragments. If it can't find an existing fragment to fit a specific slot in the structure, it calls up a general strategy to adapt the fragments until they slot into place. MINSTREL also introduces explicit elements of suspense, tragedy, and characterization to liven up the plot. Its stories have a moral and some suspense.

MINSTREL, developed in the early 1990s, was a landmark in computer-based story generation. Turner designed it to mimic human creativity, based on an author recalling interesting snippets from past stories and adapting them to fit into a new story that has both a moral and a structure.

THE MISTAKEN KNIGHT

It was the spring of 1089, and a knight named Lancelot returned to Camelot from elsewhere. Lancelot was hot tempered. Once, Lancelot had lost a joust. Because he was hot tempered, Lancelot wanted to destroy his sword. Lancelot struck his sword. His sword was destroyed.

One day, a lady of the court named Andrea wanted to have some berries. Andrea wanted to be near the woods. Andrea moved to the woods. Andrea was at the woods. Andrea had some berries because Andrea picked some berries. Lancelot's horse moved Lancelot to the woods. This unexpectedly caused him to be near Andrea. Because Lancelot was near Andrea, Lancelot loved Andrea. Some time later, Lancelot's horse moved Lancelot to the woods unintentionally, again

causing him to be near Andrea. Lancelot knew that Andrea
kissed with a knight named Frederick because Lancelot saw
that Andrea kissed with Frederick. Lancelot believed that
Andrea loved Frederick. Lancelot loved Andrea. Because
Lancelot loved Andrea, Lancelot wanted to be the love of
Andrea. But he could not because Andrea loved Frederick.
Lancelot hated Frederick. Andrea loved Frederick.
Because Lancelot was hot tempered, Lancelot wanted to
kill Frederick. Lancelot wanted to be near Frederick.
Lancelot moved to Frederick. Lancelot was near Frederick.
Lancelot fought with Frederick. Frederick was dead.

Andrea wanted to be near Frederick. Andrea moved to
Frederick. Andrea was near Frederick. Andrea told Lancelot
that Andrea was siblings with Frederick. Lancelot
believed that Andrea was siblings with Frederick.
Lancelot wanted to take back that he wanted to kill
Frederick. But he could not because Frederick was dead.
Lancelot hated himself. Lancelot became a hermit.
Frederick was buried in the woods. Andrea became a nun.

MORAL: Done in haste is done forever.

You can see the plot generator of MINSTREL churning away, moving the story forward in slow, ponderous steps, such as "Lancelot knew that Andrea kissed with a knight named Frederick because Lancelot saw that Andrea kissed with Frederick". The story has tellability, but it doesn't flow. As a reader, you don't feel that the narrative carries you along.

There's scope for a program that combines all the ideas described so far: a story grammar plus a detailed list of contrasting characters along with their attributes and a set of plans and counter-plans to cause actions and produce conflict. The Grandmother program was written in the mid-1990s by Imogen Casebourne. It is far less celebrated than MINSTREL but nicely demonstrates the main elements of a story generating program.[11]

First, the program asks the human user to set some parameters for the story. Should it be friendly or hostile? If it's hostile, should the characters be motivated by greed, revenge or hearsay? What should be the goal of the main character? What are the names of the characters? The program could just choose at random from these options, but the Grandmother program shows in a rudimentary way how a program and a human can work together to create a story.

A story grammar provides the basic engine to drive Grandmother, producing the outline of a story which the program fleshes out with text. Then, a planning system fills in the gaps. It takes a character's goal, specified by the grammar (such as "kill the murderer of my husband"), and tries to achieve it by acting out a plan. The efforts of the character to meet the goal are inserted into the outline. You can see the workings of the planner in italics. Since the planner is designed to satisfy the character's goal, which in this case is to carry out revenge against the loss of her spouse, the story can reach a conclusion with "So Emma finally got what she wanted. Which shows that ruthlessness and violence prevail over weakness".

```
** Would you like a friendly or hostile story

? hostile

** You have chosen hostile, possible motives
are . . . greed revenge hearsay

? revenge

** You have chosen revenge as a motive,
possible goals are spouse, dwelling_place

? spouse

** Possible subjects are Rebekka Deborah
Gail Yolanda Anna Agatha Emma Helen

? Emma

** You have requested a story in the hostile mode, about
revenge. The subject of this story will be Emma and her
quest for revenge following the loss of her spouse. The
story will come to a successful conclusion. Are you happy
with this story outline? Yes or no.

? Yes

** Once upon a time there was a queen called Emma who
lived in a city called Atlantis. She had lived there
happily for many years, but then one day a villager called
Rebekka came to her city and killed her husband. Filled
with hatred for Rebekka, Emma thirsted for revenge. She
resolved to hurt Rebekka. Emma wondered how she might go
about achieving her goal. She thought for a long time and
```

eventually came up with a plan. She decided to find Rebekka and murder her. However in order to kill Rebekka, Emma would need an army. Rebekka was a powerful villager, but she was vulnerable to an army. Luckily Emma already had an army, so she could embark immediately on her quest. *Emma prepared to set off on her quest but first Emma looked for Rebekka in Atlantis, however she didn't find her there. Emma sailed from Atlantis to the sea. Emma sailed from the sea to Noone. Emma looked for Rebekka in Noone, however she didn't find her there. Emma rode through the forest. This part of the forest was dark, Emma was a little scared. Emma looked for Rebekka in the forest, however she didn't find her there. Emma continued to ride through the forest. This part of the forest was green and pleasant. Emma looked for Rebekka in the forest, however she didn't find her there. Emma rode from the forest to Chilbolton. Emma looked for Rebekka in Chilbolton, and Emma found Rebekka in Chilbolton. Emma ordered her army to attack Rebekka. Rebekka received a mortal wound and died immediately.* So Emma finally got what she wanted. Which shows that ruthlessness and violence prevail over weakness. The end.

That's it? Story generating programs can write simple tales of cunning and revenge.

That's the end of the first period of computers as storytellers; then it gets more peculiar and complicated. By the start of the 1990s, three books had been published that were claimed to have been written by computers. First off the press, in 1980, was *Bagabone, Hem 'I Die Now*, a book-length story of infidelity, kidnapping and cultural discovery on a South Pacific island.[12] The book reads like a parody of romance fiction, with a meandering plot and characters drowning in treacle ("Gazing at the canopy of stars beyond the balcony, he retreated into the void of his own loneliness"). It would have gone entirely unnoticed, had the book cover not stated:

> And yet – as astounding, as unbelievable as it may seem – the *Melpomene*, identified as the author of the novel, is a *computer*. (Yes, a computer and for some details, see "about the author" on the back flap.)

Next came *The Policeman's Beard Is Half Constructed*, a book of whimsical musings from Racter, a program coded on a hobbyist computer.[13] These brief ramblings led a review in *Scientific American* to opine that Racter "speaks convincingly of its own mental world" and *The New York Times* to suggest that computers might take over the task of writing soap operas.[14] In response, some computer experts pointed out that there is a huge gap to be filled between generating catchy sentences and creating soap operas.

Then, in 1993 came the first novel that was a genuine collaboration between human and machine. *Just This Once* is a 350-page romance in the style of bestselling author Jacqueline Susann, written by a program named Hal and its programmer Scott French. French had succeeded in capturing the style of Susann, embedding it in code and calling on the code to generate a complete novel in the same style.[15]

Does that mean any novelist can capture their style in a computer program, then get it to write new books in the same style?

It took Scott French eight years to design a program that would imitate the style of one author, Jacqueline Susann. For the next quarter century a few researchers in computers and creativity looked for ways to design more powerful programs that would work like human authors, planning, drafting and revising well-formed stories.

Here's the twist. In 2019, the OpenAI company formed by entrepreneurs including Elon Musk released the complete code for a computer neural network, GPT-2, that can imitate *any* author's style without the need for expert programming.[16] Give GPT-2 the first sentence of George Orwell's novel *Nineteen Eighty-Four*, and the computer carries on in a similar dystopian vein (but set in an American diner rather than a futuristic London):

> **It was a bright cold day in April, and the clocks were striking thirteen.** We were sitting at a table in a diner just outside of Providence, Rhode Island. The television was on and we were talking about how the end of the world would come, and our possible places of exile. The burgers were thin, the mustard was dry, and the Brussels sprouts were burnt. But it was clear something was wrong. Shortly thereafter, Sam (my roommate) called in sick to work at a construction site where a road was being constructed and returned to his car, to find it running

GPT-2 has not been told the principles of creative writing, yet it seems to know how to start a story. It establishes the setting ("a diner just outside of Providence"), has a consistent narrative voice ("we were sitting", "we were talking"),[17] introduces characters ("my roommate"), creates the sense of a world out of kilter ("it was clear something was wrong"), and launches into an account of Sam returning to his car to find it running. All this from just one sentence as a prompt.

In 2020, the company revealed an even more powerful version, handily named GPT-3. At this point OpenAI suddenly became less open.[18] It didn't release the code as it had for the previous version, but licensed exclusive use of it to Microsoft. OpenAI also allowed a few selected companies and academics to access its software. One company advertises a service for writers to "generate content on diverse subjects even if they don't have prior knowledge".[19] Another lets copywriters create marketing copy in seconds.[20]

That's scary! Who needs professional writers when a computer can create a story in seconds?

You should be worried. GPT-3 and programs like it are starting to take over routine writing tasks like composing blogs and writing news stories. They are good at summarizing magazine articles and academic papers. They can write convincing poetry. The computer games industry is adopting these programs to offer lifelike characters, with personalities and emotions, who can engage in deep conversation with players.[21]

For all its power in imitating a writer's style, GPT-3 suffers from the same fundamental weaknesses as TAILOR and TALE-SPIN – it has no common-sense knowledge of the world and cannot read what it writes. A human author can plan the outline of a story, consider the traits of characters and how they interact, reflect on how the work has progressed so far, and make wholesale revisions and deletions. A neural network language generator can't do any of that. Nor can it explain its inner workings in human terms. If – and this is a big if – a program can be designed to generate a cunning plot, compose in a consistent style, check and change the story as it goes, and express this in imaginative language, then it would be a threat to human wordsmiths or a powerful new tool for creative writing.

Many writers will be repelled by the idea of sharing their craft with a computer, just as some hate style checkers and synonym prompts – anything that impedes the flow of words. What's different is that the new tools will be designed to increase the flow, to help a writer keep going. They will be writers' assistants that share ideas, show multiple ways to continue, and draw on the entire internet – including every book available online – for inspiration.

As well as offering tools for writers, story machines can probe the mystery of human creativity. For a researcher in AI, building a computer model of story writing is a grand challenge. It shows how ideas, language and experience mesh together to create stories that entertain and inspire. When a computer-generated story succeeds in engaging a reader, the program offers a possible mechanism for how we write stories. When the model fails to produce tellable tales, we are left with greater respect for the power of the human imagination and a new search for explanations of human creativity. We make the machines that make the stories that make us.

This book opens up story machines to see how they work and what they tell us about creativity and story writing. We explore three routes to designing successful story machines that work like human writers. The first, in Chapters 3 to 6, is to build *language generators* that can craft a coherent text with a beginning, middle and end, containing complications and resolutions. The second, in Chapter 7, is to create rich *storyworlds* with believable characters who have goals, motivations, desires and emotions, then let these characters tell their experiences as stories. The third and most ambitious (in Chapters 8 and 9), is to build a *working model of a storyteller* – to take what we know about how people write and code it into a program that acts like the mind of a creative author.

These methods aren't exclusive. Sometime soon, computer programs may be able to write stories with rich settings, convincing plots and compelling prose. Computer games companies may merge with media studios to produce automated sitcoms where you can engage in witty banter with the cast or immersive dramas where you can guide a character through bloody battles and tense negotiations. Artificially intelligent bards may sing ballads of their life in the worldwide web. Technology companies could offer new tools to teach story writing and take over when you get blocked. These won't come just from building more powerful supercomputers that crunch texts from the internet and imitate a writer's style. To take the next big step, AI researchers, cognitive scientists and storytellers will need to work together on understanding how the creative mind works and how to tell a good story.

Human story machines   **2**

Your brain sits inside its skull, dark and silent. The only way you can get information about the outside world is through your eyes, ears, nose, mouth and skin. But these signals arrive at different times. For example, your brain perceives colour about 80 milliseconds before it registers motion. It picks up locations before colours, colours before orientation. Yet it has a remarkable facility to smooth out these discrepancies and discontinuities to give you a feeling of continuity, of events happening in a smooth, orderly manner.[1]

Try this exercise. Go up to a mirror and look at your left eye. Then shift your gaze to your right eye, then back to your left eye. It all seems perfectly natural. But wait, you never see your eyes moving! It's not that it happens too quickly, because you can easily see another person's eyes moving from side to side. Without you being aware, your brain has smoothed over the gap in time when your gaze goes from one eye to another. It is the same facility that makes the world seem stable even though your gaze is continually shifting from one object to another. Your brain forms a story about the world outside.[2] You are a story machine, making sense of a fragmented experience by understanding and creating stories.

Wired for stories

Whatever the level of analysis, we find that humans are wired for stories. At the neural level, the brain assembles bits of experience into a coherent sequence. There's a part of the human brain named Broca's area that coordinates speech and movement. In one study, Patrik Fazio and colleagues

DOI: 10.4324/9781003161431-2

showed short movies to patients who had damage to the Broca's area of their brains.[3] Then they presented these people with four still pictures from each movie, in random order. The patients were generally able to say which picture came before or after another one but found it harder to put all four pictures into the correct sequence. Interestingly, the brain-damaged patients only failed to order the pictures of human actions (such as a person grasping a bottle) – they were able to carry out the task for pictures of physical objects (such as a bicycle falling over). It seems that this region of the brain constructs narratives by imitating inside the brain the sequence of human actions that the eyes and ears perceive.

At a cognitive level, stories are how we make continuous sense of the world. We recall the past and plan the future not as discrete events, but as a connected sequence. Let's say you and a friend are discussing the quickest way to get from her home to yours. You might suggest a route and discuss whether to take a shorter road with traffic or a longer but less congested journey. You and your friend are not recalling an actual journey but creating a mutual narrative of how to get from one home to another. To do that depends on having a shared causal reality – agreeing how the world is constructed and how to choose the route that makes driving easiest.

And as social beings, we seek out stories that fit our view of the world. We generally join social networks not to challenge our ideas but to confirm them. Together with many others we create bubbles of self-affirming conformity. If some event comes along that challenges this shared view, instead trying to accommodate it, we cast it aside as not fitting into the story. As we write this book, there is a debate in the UK news about whether to wear a face covering during the COVID-19 pandemic. It isn't a rational scientific argument, but two competing stories. One story is that people should have the right to decide for themselves whether to cover their faces. The other story is about how face coverings protect others, so not to wear one is selfish and dangerous. No matter what the scientific evidence, it will be co-opted into whichever story we follow.

All these elements act together. The brain merges signals from our senses to give an impression of continuous experience. That experience is laid down as narrative memories. The memories form our view of the past as a continuous personal story that we can tell to ourselves and others. We can use the same mental processes to plan the future and to create fantasies about other worlds.

Learning by storytelling

The ability to tell and understand the world through stories starts at a young age. Children find their place in the world and discover other worlds through storytelling. They learn how events connect together, how to describe what happened during the day, how to create fantasies, and how to distinguish reality from fiction. If children had to learn about the everyday world through analysis and reasoning rather by following stories, it would be a slow and painful process.

Here is a transcribed voice recording I (Mike) made of two girls, age 7.[4] They are playing with a toy model of a windmill. It has a winch at the front with a string and a hook on it to wind up miniature sacks of flour into the loft at the top of the windmill. The girls have decided that the windmill is the venue for a party. We join their conversation as they hook toy guests onto the winch and wind them up into the loft:

Elaine: They've come to the party too, haven't they?

Lucy: No, not all of them are grown ups. Most of them are children, including him.

Elaine: Including what?

Lucy: Him. He's a child.

Elaine: No he isn't. He's a big grown-up.

Lucy: But he isn't going to the party.

Elaine: No, because he's too old.

Lucy: Everything's going OK.

Elaine: Should be pull . . . oops! [Giggles]

Elaine: He's saying, "My darling. I want you to snog me."

Lucy: He gets up and then. He gets up and says, "Now you kids. Now what are you kids playing at?" And he gets hooked in the back. [Giggles]

The girls are immersed in the storyworld of a party at the windmill. In that short section of play conversation, they decide on the characters ("most of them are children"), then start to build a plot around who goes to the party and who doesn't. They add some adult dialogue ("My darling, I want you to snog me"). And they introduce comedic tension when the adult doll, in the middle of addressing the children, gets hooked in the back and lifted into the air. The two children are creating a shared story through their actions and conversation.

Telling stories about our activities seems perfectly normal. How could it be otherwise? Remember the anxiety of taking exams. Those exam questions were designed to challenge you to write analytic essays rather than personal narratives, to find sources of information to justify statements rather than tell anecdotes, to solve problems from fundamental principles rather than access previous experience. School education is designed to push children out of story mode into reasoning and analysis. But here's the rub – people find it easier to understand and remember information presented as stories compared to academic explanations. A recent paper surveyed 37 studies that compared learning from stories or from explanations – it found a clear advantage for learning through storytelling.[5] Educational story books, such as *Sir Cumference and the First Round Table*, *Deena's Lucky Penny* and *Beetle Boy*, are engaging ways to teach school subjects.

Because young children learn about the world beyond them from storytelling, it makes sense to introduce topics in maths, science and history through stories. In the words of Rudyard Kipling: "If history were taught in the form of stories, it would never be forgotten".[6] Kipling would have loved the book *What did the tree see?* that follows the story of an oak tree as it witnesses life over hundreds of years. That's not to say all school topics should be taught as stories – there's a clear need for children to learn facts and formulas and to practice solving problems – but storytelling captures children's interest, connects events over time, and shows how abstract topics such as probability operate in the real world.

Living through stories

As we mature, we turn our actions in the world into stories, and the stories we tell ourselves are the basis for future action. It's a cyclical process of acting and telling. Not only do we tell stories *about* our lived experience; we live *through* stories. Our actions are constrained by the stories we can and can't tell. We think and act through stories that make our sense of reality seem natural and connected. We have become human story machines. When the world doesn't match the everyday narrative, it is strange and uncomfortable, like the dislocating experience of going to a foreign country for the first time, where taking a train journey or eating a meal in a café doesn't quite follow our familiar script.

In the 1970s, Roger Schank and colleagues at Yale proposed that we all have mental representations – which they named scripts – that influence how we act in familiar settings such as restaurants or meetings.[7] Schank argued that mental scripts guide how we perform our way through social situations in daily life. They form the basis of our personal narratives. He and his students showed the power of scripts by embedding them into computer programs to understand and generate stories.[8] This led some people to propose that our minds work like computers interpreting mental data structures. But a human isn't commanded by mental scripts like a musical box playing a never-ending tune as the drum rotates. Schankian mental scripts are more like ways of acting, shaped by experience and by being told stories of how to behave in different settings. They are highly bound up with context: we act differently in a busy restaurant than we do at an informal dinner party.

When we suddenly need to behave in new ways (such as in a pandemic where we have to keep social distancing in crowded spaces) it's not that we amend our mental rule books; rather we try out new ways of acting, and these become part of our everyday practice. We share stories with friends about our strange new behaviours until they become part of a new routine and no longer worth talking about.

Evolution of storytelling

When we can't try a new situation for ourselves, we rely on professional storytellers to take us there. In the modern world, the storytellers that form our behaviour appear on CNN, BBC, Fox News and internet streams. Whichever channel we follow sets our overarching narrative. If news channels have been so important in forming opinion, how did societies tell stories before TV or newspapers? How did storytelling arise, and why are we so attuned to stories? New research into the evolution of language suggests just how much we are creatures of narrative.[9]

What follows is one theory among many, but it addresses the question of why humans are so well adapted to living through stories. It starts, like most accounts of the origins of human language, with animal communication and what makes human verbal interaction different from how animals communicate. The suggestion is not that humans invented language, then began to tell stories, but the reverse: human language evolved from storytelling.

In this account, it is the ability to narrate a connected series of events that happened in the past and to tell stories of the future that sets humans apart from other animals. Other species can remember past events and even refer to them (for example, an orangutan named Kikan was recorded acting out an event that happened a week earlier when his caregiver removed a splinter from his foot),[10] but only humans have been seen to engage in what has been called "mental time travel" – to communicate by taking another person through a series of events from the past.

Humans as mental time travellers have a superpower not possessed by other species: an ability to detach from the present, to recount events from the past, and to foretell the future. A mental time traveller is an entertainer, a planner and a prophet.

If human language evolved from this cognitive ability to re-enact the past and foresee the future, then what came before? How did people tell stories before the advent of language? The suggestion is that verbal language isn't needed for storytelling. Our early ancestors told stories by acting out sequences of past events – the first storytellers were mime artists. They needn't have been silent. There would probably have been much grunting, squeaking, roaring and cheering involved, but the continuing narrative would have been communicated through actions.

Over millennia, language evolved to give expression to the actions, then became a substitute for them. Mime, cave paintings, shadow puppets and silent movies can all tell stories without spoken language, but the verbalization brings subtlety and nuance. Mime acting was the bridge between being able to communicate events from the past and evolving spoken language.

The structure of language makes it easy to tell simple stories. There's no need to build a linguistic structure in advance of telling. Even young children can form stories by stringing together with "then" or "next" sentences that describe past actions: we went to the shops, then mummy bought me an ice cream, then we played in the park, then we came home, and so on. As stories become more sophisticated, with flashbacks and digressions, so language has evolved to cope through tenses and more complex sentence structures.

The power of a story

If storytelling is a superpower of prehistoric times, able to take listeners back to the past and forward to the future, then it follows that good storytellers would have a special place in early communities. In a fascinating study of the Agta people, indigenous nomadic communities in the Philippines, anthropologists looked at the role of storytellers in these contemporary hunter-gatherer societies.[11] First, they asked three elders to narrate stories they typically tell to their children and each other. Here is one such story, summarized in English by the researchers:

> Wild pig and seacow were best friends and always raced each other for fun. But the seacow injured his legs and could not run anymore. The wild pig was unhappy and carried the seacow to the sea. They could race each other again, pig on the land and seacow in the sea.

From these and many other stories the researchers gathered at hunter-gatherer communities, they found that the most-told tales were about how to cooperate and support others in the community. Some stories told how to treat people equally, some were about accepting those who looked or behaved differently, some showed the value of friendship. Those Agta camps with a greater proportion of storytellers were the most cooperative.

Not only were the storytellers effective in building cooperation, they were also popular. The researchers asked other people in the camp to choose who they would most like to live with. Storytellers came out top, in front of skilled hunters and fishers. The researchers even found that that the storytellers had, on average, more children than other camp members. As the study concludes: storytellers make good mates.

Epic tales

It seems that through the ages and across societies people desire to be told, in entertaining ways, how to behave. These stories have survived as fairy tales with morals such as "don't stray into the woods" and "be careful who you trust." As societies grew in size, so did the stories. Epic tales of travel and adventure, conflicts among gods and warriors, and battles between powerful enemies were the stuff of stories passed down through generations and eventually preserved on clay tablets, then paper. The characters in these epic tales became emblems of power and morality, struggles between civilization and nature, comradeship and cowardice, right and wrong.

The Epic of Gilgamesh is one of the oldest surviving epic poems.[12] It dates from 2100 BCE and was recorded on baked clay tablets. While Gilgamesh heralds later epics, from the Iliad to Frankenstein and Star Wars, it also retains elements of the morality tales from smaller communities. It tells the story of Gilgamesh – part man, part god, King of Uruk – who befriends Enkidu, a wild man who has lived among animals. Gilgamesh and Enkidu embark on adventures to defeat enemies. They kill a divine bull sent by Ishtar, goddess of love, after Gilgamesh rejects her marriage proposal. The gods inflict a disease on Enkidu to punish him. Fearing his own death, Gilgamesh visits the sage Utnapishtim, only survivor of a great flood, hoping to become immortal. Gilgamesh fails in the tasks set by Utnapishtim and returns home to Uruk, still mortal.

Four thousand years later, Gilgamesh still retains the power to generate sensational stories. One original tablet from the epic, now in the British Museum, tells of the meeting with Utnapishtim. It caused a storm in the 19th century because of its similarity to the Flood story written later in the book of Genesis.[13] And in a further bizarre twist as we write this chapter, Hobby Lobby, a US arts and crafts company, is suing the auction house Christie's for selling to the company another ancient tablet from the Epic of Gilgamesh that had allegedly been smuggled out of Iraq. The tablet was seized from Hobby Lobby by the US government, leaving the company $1.6 million poorer.[14]

Modern epics

In modern times, epic stories have been mechanized to preserve them and enhance their power to captivate, but they have kept the same structure found in Gilgamesh of a flawed hero who is challenged, goes on adventures, tries to overcome danger, fails, finally succeeds, and ends wiser but unsatisfied.

Umberto Eco wrote a penetrating essay called "The Narrative Structure in Fleming".[15] In it, he showed that Ian Fleming's novels of James Bond are built around a series of contrasts between characters and values, such as Bond–M, Bond–Villain, Villain–Woman, love–death, luxury–discomfort, loyalty–disloyalty. He set out 14 of these "oppositions" which, Eco suggested, include all of Fleming's narrative ideas. For example, in the contract between Bond and his boss M, there is a "dominated-dominant relationship which characterizes from the beginning the limits and possibilities of the character of Bond and sets events moving". The plots of all the Bond novels can be seen as games with the opposing pieces, governed by fixed rules and moves. The scheme of moves is as follows:

A. M moves and gives a task to Bond.
B. The Villain moves and appears to Bond (perhaps in alternative forms).
C. Bond moves and gives a first check to the Villain or the Villain gives a first check to Bond.
D. The Woman moves and shows herself to Bond.
E. Bond seduces the Woman.
F. The Villain captures Bond (with or without the Woman).
G. The Villain tortures Bond (with or without the Woman).
H. Bond conquers the Villain (kills him, or kills his representative, or helps in their killing).
I. Bond convalescing enjoys time with the Woman, whom he then loses.

Although the scheme is fixed in the sense that all the elements are present in every novel, the order may change. In *Dr. No* the order is A B C D E F G H I, but for *Goldfinger* it is B C D E A C D F G D H E H I.

As Eco concluded, it is clear how the James Bond novels attained such a wide success. They translate the purity and order of epic stories into current terms and transform a network of elementary associations into new but familiar patterns. Each story encapsulates what is tellable, what moves an audience, what is right and wrong. It is told from the perspective of the teller and many tellers before that.

Internet heroes

In the age of the internet, fact and fantasy have become hopelessly intertwined. Richard Branson, Elon Musk and Jeff Bezos compete for the role of archetypal flawed hero, launching into physical space in their cars, rockets and spaceplanes and into cyberspace through music streaming and Bitcoin. The Tony Stark character in the Iron Man movies was modelled in part on the entrepreneur Elon Musk. In *Iron Man 2*, Musk had a cameo part, playing himself. Some scenes for that movie were filmed at Musk's SpaceX facility.[16] As their epic adventures are played out across multiple media, these heroes are bound by the stories they tell and are told about them.

On a smaller but no less mesmerizing scale, internet influencers create modern myths on social media. They weave stories of magical potions and supernatural powers, of conspiracies and triumphs, of new products and rituals. Influencers such as Furong Jiejie (Sister Furong) in China and Emma Chamberlain in the US, have become internet stars by telling of their transformation through dance, makeup and clothing.[17]

That does not mean human storytellers are bound to culture and convention, playing to the scripts demanded by brand managers and internet followers. The modern heroes and influencers are continually pushing the bounds of what can be said and done. Branson, Musk, Bezos and other billionaire adventurers regularly go off script, confounding their supporters and critics. Internet influencers gain followers by setting new trends. Disrupting familiar scripts, such as the friendly meeting in a restaurant, has inspired some great movie scenes: the café full of young people bombed in *Battle of Algiers*; the street that explodes around the bistro in *Inception*; the restaurant assassination in *The Godfather*; the faked orgasm at Katz's Deli in *When Harry Met Sally*. To invent such disruptions is truly creative.

Humans as story machines are not automatons tracing a pre-written program. Rather, storytelling is constrained by the traditional forms of epic and myth, by the structures of language, by the conventions of scripts that guide how to behave in familiar situations, and by a flow of events that resonate with the reader's mental construction of narrative. Any writer can break these constraints for creative effect, but no writer can ignore them.

Creativity mechanized

Professional writers throughout the ages have been fascinated by the mechanization of creativity and how this might be embedded in composing engines. In ancient Rome, the poet Virgil wrote of a priestess, the Sybil of Cumae, who lived in a dark cave. She wrote prophecies as individual words on oak leaves which she laid in the cave's entrance.[18] When a blast of wind came, the leaves would fly into the air and fall scattered on the ground where visitors had to gather them up and interpret the wisdom as best they could.

The twin concepts of randomness and completeness lie behind story generation systems from ancient times until the present day. From controlling randomness comes creativity. From completeness arises exhaustion and infinity. A machine to constrain the random generation of letters, words or plots – and do so over and over again – might embody the essence of a creative mind.

In the book *Gulliver's Travels*, first published in 1726, Lemuel Gulliver visits an Academy dedicated to running bizarre and pointless experiments, such as extracting sunbeams from cucumbers and turning human excrement back into food.[19] One part of the Academy is for "Advancers of speculative learning". There Gulliver finds a large machine, 20 feet square, in the shape of a table with 40 iron handles arranged around its sides. On the tabletop are square blocks of wood, each showing a word. A professor describes the machine as a "contrivance [whereby] the most ignorant person, at a reasonable charge, and with a little bodily labour, might write books in philosophy, poetry, politics, laws, mathematics, and theology, without the least assistance from genius or study".

Forty pupils stand in ranks around the sides of the frame. The professor asks Gulliver to observe as he sets the engine to work. At his command the pupils take hold of the iron handles and give them a sudden turn. The blocks shift over to display new words. The professor then commands lads to read the lines of words softly, as they appear on the frame. When the pupils find three or four words together that might make part of a sentence, they dictate these to other boys, who write them down. This is repeated, again and again, with the engine shifting the words into new places as the square bits of wood move upside down. The words aren't quite produced at random, since the professor has added them to the machine in the strict proportions of nouns, verbs and other parts of speech found in books.

The professor shows Gulliver several volumes of broken sentences that he intends to piece together so as to give the world a complete body of all arts and sciences. The project would be much improved if only the public would raise a fund to build five hundred such frames to speed the work.

Later novelists followed Jonathan Swift in mocking the efforts of scientists to build all-powerful writing machines while realizing how their craft is already mechanized by technology (pens, paper, typewriters) and constrained by language and convention. Even the celebrated author Sir Walter Scott got in on the act. In *Tales of the Crusadors*, written in 1825, Scott describes a fictional eccentric German genius, Hermann Dousterswivel, who has invented a steam-driven machine to automate the writing of commonplace bits of prose "such as the love-speeches of the hero, the description of the heroine's person, the moral observations of all sorts, and the distribution of happiness at the end of the piece".[20] The human author tired of pumping his own brain can relax his fingers and let the machine take over.

In 1953, at the dawn of the electronic computer age, Roald Dahl wrote a short story in an anthology for teenagers.[21] "The Great Automatic Grammatizator" tells the tale of a young computer engineer, Adolph Knipe, who is working on a government project to build a computer. Instead of being pleased that the new computing engine is able to carry out rapid mathematical calculations, he goes home dispirited, pours a glass of whisky, and stares at a half-finished sheet of typing. For, in his spare time, Adolph is a writer of stories that he has tried to get published in magazines, without any success.

Suddenly, Adolph gets an idea. Why not program the computer to do the writing. If it can compute mathematical functions, it could also generate short stories. He codes thousands of words, plots of stories, extracts from *Roget's Thesaurus*, surnames. He also designs a control panel to select the type of magazine, from *Reader's Digest* to *Ladies Home Journal*. The short story generator works. It spews out hundreds of short stories that Adolph and his manager Mr Bohlen sell to magazines for a tidy fortune.

Buoyed by their success and their income, Adolph and Mr Bohlen decide to go for the big challenge – to extend the story machine to produce novels. Two months later, the machine has sprouted buttons, pedals and dials designed for novel writing. Sitting at the console, like a pilot in an aircraft, the author can pre-select any type of plot and writing style, then operate the machine as it writes by viewing dials, pressing pedals, pushing buttons and pulling out stops, as on an organ. These control the elements of story writing such as tension, surprise, humour, pathos and mystery.

After a failed attempt where the machine's output shows an excess of the "passion" element, the pair manage to get it under control. They create a manuscript and sell it to an enthusiastic publisher as the work of a promising new writer. They then set up their own literary agency and decide to buy out famous novelists – persuading them to sign a contract for an income for life in return for secrecy and their names being used on novels generated by the Automatic Grammatizator. As the secret spreads, famous novelists rush to sign up for a lifetime of leisure created by the great machine. The story ends with the penniless writer of this story sitting at his desk listening to the howling of his nine starving children, his hand creeping closer to that golden contract.

Many other well-known writers including Isaac Asimov, Arthur C Clarke, J. G. Ballard, Michael Frayn and George Orwell have been captivated and repelled by the thought that one day a machine will take over storytelling, reducing it to programmed alignments of symbols.[22] For some, this expresses a writer's angst that they have themselves become writing machines, at the will of some internal force that they can't control. As the author William S. Burroughs put it, "I am a recording instrument. . . . Insofar as I succeed in direct recording of certain areas of psychic process I may have limited function".[23] The Italian journalist and writer Italo Calvino went further in his essay "Cybernetics and Ghosts", to claim that the so-called personality of the writer is the product and the instrument of the writing process. When composing is successful, the writer disappears and the writing process takes over. If we can replicate that process in a computer, Calvino suggests, then the spoiled human author vanishes to give place to a more thoughtful person "who will know that the author is a machine, and will know how this machine works".[24]

Although these authors fantasized about the machine as a writer and the writer as a machine, none of them were driven to build an actual creativity engine. That work began with a grocer in a small town in 19th-century England.

Artificial versifying   **3**

The Egyptian Hall in London's Piccadilly was an imposing building. Built in 1812 to look like an Egyptian temple, its façade was covered in hieroglyphics. Visitors entered below two huge statues, supposedly of the Egyptian gods Isis and Osiris. Originally intended as a museum of natural history, the building evolved over the 19th century to become an exhibition hall and theatre. Its exhibits included French paintings, Tyrolian minstrels, a live Welsh dwarf, and a huge model of the Battle of Waterloo.[1]

In 1845, leaflets were handed out advertising "The Eureka, a machine for making Latin verses" to be exhibited daily at The Egyptian Hall, with illustrative lectures. For the price of one shilling, visitors to the exhibition could view a large cabinet that looked like a bookcase on legs, with six long, thin horizontal slots at eye height.[2] On pulling a lever, letters appeared in the slots and arranged themselves, as if by magic, into Latin words that formed gloomy and portentous sentences, such as:

MARTIA CASTRA FORIS PRÆNARRANT PROELIA MULTA

which roughly translates as "Martial encampments foretell many oppositions abroad". Each pull of the lever produced a new line of Latin. To add to the effect, as the letters appeared one by one, the machine played the national anthem and projected a kaleidoscopic light show onto the ceiling.

DOI: 10.4324/9781003161431-3

A new way to make Latin verses

The idea of a Latin verse machine began in the 17th century. In 1677, a mathematician named John Peter published a booklet with the title "Artificial Versifying, or the Schoolboy's Recreation: A new way to make Latin verses".[3] He claimed on the title page that anyone of ordinary capacity who knows only the ABCs and can count to nine could produce hundreds of true Latin verses.

The booklet contained six tables of letters that gave a cipher to generate the Latin text. They are shown here in modern type.

1

i	s	a	t	t	h	t	p	p	m	o
s	u	r	o	u	e	e	p	r	p	r
i	r	r	s	r	i	d	e	b	s	r
p	s	f	a	i	r	i	t	i	i	i
i		d	a	d	i	d	a	m	d	b
a		a	a	a		a	a	b		b
		b								

2

d	f	f	b	i	v	v	d	d	i	a
a	e	u	o	e	o	a	c	c	t	l
r	t	r	n	m	t	t	a	l	a	a
b	a	n	a	a		a			a	
a			b		b	i		b		

3

m	t	i	v	m	v	r	a	s	i	i
n	i	a	i	e	l	c	h	b	q	r
l	d	o	i	i	i	i	u	o	i	e
r	i	o			a		s	s		s
	b	r	m	b			b			r
b										

4

p	p	m	p	p	c	c	p	c	r	r
o	o	r	a	o	r	o	æ	o	n	r
o	u	n	o	n	d	c	s	t	m	s
c	d	f	i	u	t	a	i	a	e	u
i	c	r	r	b	t	b	d	c	r	u
a	a	u	t	u	u	u	m	n	n	b
n	u	n	n	n	a	t	t	u	t	n
t	t	t	n			n		t		
	t	b	b	t	r		b	r	b	
b	b									

5

s	s	p	f	c	t	d	i	p	i
o	i	œ	r	e	o	u	o	d	m
g	d	i	m	g	r	c	e	n	n
e	m	p	m	g	u	r	i	o	r
i	o	a	i	l	a	a	r	a	n
r	t	a	a		a			a	a
a			b	r		b			

6

m	q	c	t	p	s	p	s	s	u	u
e	a	l	o	r	e	æ	l	æ	r	n
a	l	a	m	p	t	d	t	t	n	a
v	p	e	a	a	a	u	e		a	e
		m		m		b		r	r	b
	b		d	b	r					

The booklet also had 14 pages of instructions on how to operate these tables that are about as penetrable as the manual for a microwave oven. In his defence, Peter was one of the first people to attempt to write an instruction manual in an era when pamphlets were mainly for religious sermons or political propaganda. Here's our attempt to rewrite his 14 pages of instructions as a step-by-step guide so you can amaze your friends with your ability to create Latin verse (don't worry if you can't follow them; it's not essential):

1   Write down any six digits from 1 to 9 to form a six-digit number, for example: 467182. Each digit is the key to one of the tables. So, 4 is the key to Table 1, 6 is the key to Table 2, etc.
2   For the first digit (4 in the example), count forward along the top row of Table 1 until you reach the number 9. For the example, that's the letter "t" in Table 1 (the fifth letter along the top row). Write that down as the first letter of your verse. [Note: Whenever you choose the digit 9, then count the first letter in the table as 1, the second 2, and so on till you reach 9, then write down that letter.]
3   Keep going along the row, counting from 1 up to 9. When you get to the end of a row, start at the beginning of the row below. For the example, from the letter "t" in the top row, count along the top row and then the row below until you reach the ninth letter ("r"). Write that down as the next letter in your verse.
4   Keep going, counting each ninth letter until you reach a black square, then stop. In the example, that should generate the remaining letters "i", "s", "t", "i", "a", to form your first word, "tristia".
5   Do the same for the next five tables. So, for table two, the first letter in the example should be "f" (count up from 6 to 9 along the top row and write down that letter) and the remaining ones "a", "t", "a", forming "fata". The complete set of words forms a line of Latin verse: "Tristia fata tibi producunt sidera prava" (meaning "Fate will produce untoward stars").

Whichever series of six digits you choose, the tables will produce a new line of Latin, in perfect hexameter rhythm.[4]

Of course, the tables don't confer the power of Latin on schoolboys. They are an elaborate game, similar to modern word-search puzzles where words are hidden within a grid of letters. Each table hides nine words that can be found by starting from a letter on the top row and counting forward nine squares to get the next letter and so on. John Peter could have just listed the nine words for each table, but that would have ruined the mystery.

The tables are ordered according to the strictures of Latin grammar, so the words always produce grammatically correct sentences: Adjective Noun Adverb Verb Noun Adjective. Lastly, Peter carefully chose the words for each table to conform to the hexameter rhythm of classical Latin poetry.[5] The "Artificial Versifying" booklet proved popular and led to imitations of the tables over the next century.

There are various reasons why John Peter chose to create tables for Latin poetry rather than English prose. Latin is an orderly language with a regular structure to its sentences, so he could slot in many words to each table, and they would form grammatical sentences. Latin was also the language of scholars. Scientists in the 17th century were devising intricate ways to mechanize arithmetic, calculate tides, and determine the positions of planets. Why not attempt also to mechanize the process of poetry writing?

In the 17th century, wealthy parents paid large sums to give their sons an education in "the classics" based on intensive study of Latin and Greek literature. The ability to compose Latin verse in the style of Virgil and Ovid was the pinnacle of a schoolboy's study. It showed culture, good taste, and a command of language.[6] So, there's something deeply subversive in publishing tables to give any schoolboy who can follow instructions and count up to nine the ability to generate over half a million well-formed Latin verses.

The clockwork verse machine

Early Victorian England was a place of huge scientific and cultural upheaval. Novelists, including the Brontë sisters, Thackeray and Dickens, held the family and society to scrutiny. Photography created pictures from light. The People's charter advocated democratic reform. Slavery was abolished in the British Empire. The railway boom began. And the Victorian public crowded new museums and art galleries to appreciate art, science and technology.

John Clark was 52 when Victoria came to the throne.[7] He had worked as a grocer, upholsterer and printer, but his passion was invention. In 1813, he had invented and patented a method of making cloth waterproof, which he sold to Charles Macintosh who went on to manufacture the waterproof raincoat. Clark invented the world's first blow-up airbed and devised an early type of fire-escape. He also had a gift for writing poetry and wrote a long continuation of Byron's poem *Don Juan* which he published and sold. His enduring project was to build a verse machine.

For 13 years, Clark toiled to construct a machine that could automate the tables of John Peter and later artificial versifiers so that it would grind out poetry as a mill grinds flour. Even by the high standards of British eccentricity, Clark was a standout. His niece described him as looking like a "big boy", with a short jacket, short trousers and an open-necked shirt.[8] Charles Babbage, inventor of the first computing engine, met Clark and his Eureka and commented that "John Clark was as great a curiosity as his machine".[9]

Far removed from the precision engineering of Babbage's Analytical Engine, John Clark's Eureka was cobbled together from old clock workings and bits of wood and wire. Yet, unlike the products of Babbage, it worked.

The Eureka is housed in a wooden cabinet on legs, about the size of a modern washing machine. On the outside are six narrow slots to display the letters that form the Latin words. Inside are three mechanisms: a clockwork motor, six wooden cylinders with rows of metal spikes sticking out of them, and long square rods with letters from A – V marked on them that drop down to form the words.

The motor, as in a grandfather clock, is wound up by a key and put into motion by a lever. When the lever is pulled, each cylinder rotates a different amount to bring a new line of metal spikes to the top. Then, the rods slowly descend. The letters roll by the viewing slot until each rod stops on the end of its spike. Clark carefully trimmed the spikes so that each one produces a particular letter when the rod rests on it. A very long spike makes the letter A; a very short one, the letter V. The illustration shows one cylinder with the

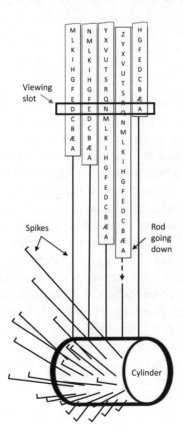

spikes forming the letters DEN_A in the viewing area. The fourth rod has not yet to come to rest, to make the Latin word DENSA.[10]

When the rods have settled, each window shows a Latin word, with all six slots forming a line of verse such as:

TURPIA DAMNA QUIDEM DECLARANT CARMINA NIGRA

which roughly translates as "shameful damage is manifested by black songs".

Like the "Artificial Versifying" tables, the words coded as spikes on each cylinder were chosen for their part of speech – adjective, noun, adverb, verb, noun, adjective – and their poetic rhythm, or metre. The machine will always produce a line of Latin that has correct grammar and metre, though it may not always make sense. What makes Eureka different from earlier automata is its generative power. The changing combinations of words mean that Eureka is able to generate 28 million different lines of Latin verse.

Hexameter mania

Eureka's daily performances in London coincided with and contributed to a curious phenomenon in Victorian England that has been called "hexameter mania". Its essence was a lively debate about teaching the traditions and languages of classical antiquity in English schools.[11] The epic poems of ancient Greece and Rome were written in a specific hexameter metre of long and short syllables. Boys in the elite schools of England were taught to read these verses in the original languages and to compose their own poems in the same style as a way of connecting with ancient cultures and their virtues of courage and self-discipline. However, by the mid-19th century this had descended into rote learning, with pupils looking up textbooks of verse composition to grind out pastiches of Ovid and Virgil. On one side of the great debate were those who saw classical education as a framework for moral and critical thinking. On the other side were those who derided the backward-looking curriculum of elite schools and universities as being totally out of touch with modern science and politics. Its echoes still rumble on in the classical education movement that advocates teaching children the traditions and languages of antiquity.[12]

The Eureka, a wooden box built by a former grocer and self-taught poet, produced line after line of well-formed yet nonsensical Latin verse, like a demented schoolboy. Why did John Clark spend 13 years of his life building a clockwork poetry machine? It was certainly not to contribute to hexameter mania, nor was it to help school pupils with their homework. Clark wanted to understand how Latin verse worked, so he designed a machine to simulate it. In his own description of the Eureka, Clark wrote [his emphasis] "The *Rules of verse . . .* which act as fetters of confinement to the *writers* of verses, much increasing their difficulties, have an *opposite effect* when applied to *a machine*".[13] By building a machine for artificial versifying, he could explore and play with the rules of Latin verse.

One hundred eighty years later, we can see John Clark as an early cognitive scientist who built a working model of creative composition. In a letter to *The Athenaeum* magazine Clark describes how his machine simulates the process of composition by forming individual letters into words through the medium of numbers (what we would now call computer code), made tangible in his machine.[14] Cognitive science builds models of minds with the most powerful technologies available. Nowadays, they are computers and AI programs. In Clark's time, the latest technology to demonstrate patterns of creativity was the newly-invented kaleidoscope – so he called his simulation of verse writing "kaleidoscopic evolution". As Clark made clear in his letter, this was only the start. The possibilities for "harmonious combination" of letters into words and words into literature are "practically interminable".

It's worth examining why Clark adopted the kaleidoscope as a model for creative composition.[15] The kaleidoscope was invented in the early 19th century as a scientific instrument. By the mid-century it was sold as a toy, but it also demonstrated how carefully aligned mirrors could form small items, such as bits of coloured glass, into beautiful orderly patterns. By analogy, the Eureka machine took individual letters of the alphabet and, through carefully-aligned drums and wires, produced line after line of orderly (though not so beautiful) Latin verse.

The drums of Eureka revolve different amounts to produce new alignments of the six cylinders. As the wooden staves (rectangular rods) with the letters slide down, they are constrained by the metal spikes so they only form Latin words. The combination of random alignment and constrained patterns is what causes creativity in both the kaleidoscope and the Eureka.

Like many inventors, Clark found that building the machine itself took much longer than expected. He was no different from some modern researchers in AI who have spent decades developing and refining programs to generate poems and stories. Happily, the exhibition of Eureka in the Egyptian Hall was a commercial success, and its proceeds funded the inventor, John Clark, into comfortable retirement.

We have described the Eureka machine in the present tense because it still exists. When John Clark died in 1853, his poetry machine passed among family members, was moved to the Clarks shoe factory in Somerset, England, and ended up at the company museum in Somerset. A recent project with the University of Exeter has restored the Eureka to working order.[16] A visit to the museum's Reading Room is a step back in time to the age of clockwork and carpentry. The photograph shows Eureka standing proud on a pedestal, its façade glowing with gold paint. Opening the front panel reveals a profusion of metal spikes sticking out from a line of drums, like an oversized hedgehog. The back panel reveals the clockwork mechanism, with ten cogwheels, weights to lift the staves then let them fall onto the spikes, and a long tube that worked like a musical box to play the national anthem. At the side is the key to wind up the device and a lever to set the machinery in motion. And most important are the six slots at eye height on the front, edged in gold. Visitors must have craned forward to see the tiny letters appear one by one and gasped as they formed a line of Latin verse.

Oulipo, or workshop of potential literature

By the end of the 19th century, John Clark and his Eureka machine had been forgotten, but his spirit of having serious fun with language lived on. In 1898, the absurdist author Alfred Jarry wrote a novel, *Gestes et Opinions du Docteur Faustroll Pataphysicien: Roman Néo-scientifique Suivi de Spéculations*, or *Exploits and Opinions of Dr. Faustroll, Pataphysician*.[17] The book was a Swiftian tale of the travels of a doctor and his companion in a copper skiff across a sea superimposed over the streets and buildings of Paris. Jarry coined the term "pataphysics" to describe a "science of imaginary solutions", such as the laws governing exceptions to rules. A College of Pataphysics was founded in Paris in 1948, dedicated to learned and useless research.[18]

There is no point in trying to give a more precise definition of pataphysics, since it was intended to be deliberately vague and playful. Its main effect has been to encourage otherwise serious men (and it has been almost entirely men) to do silly things with language.[19] In 1960, a group of writers, mathematicians and university professors met in Cerisy-la-Salle, France, to form a subcommittee of the College of Pataphysics which they called the "Ouvroir de Littérature Potentialle" (Workshop of Potential Literature) or Oulipo for short. A photograph taken in 1975 of an Oulipo meeting shows a group of 13 men and one woman sitting round a garden table studiously looking at manuscripts or engaging in learned discussion. The contrast is striking between these suave, well-groomed academics and a photograph of John Clark, alone, with wild hair, shirt open to the chest, staring wistfully into the distance.

Whereas Clark was an engineer who laboured for 13 years to build a machine that conformed to the rules of Latin verse, the Oulipians were a cultural elite who dedicated themselves to systematically testing and breaking the constraints of language. They set themselves in opposition to surrealist artists and writers who had attempted to free themselves from constraint by liberating their subconscious minds. The Oulipians embraced constraint. They sought new ways to fetter themselves as writers and so discover the true nature of creativity.

A leading member of Oulipo, George Perec, wrote a 300-page novel, *La Disparition*, without using the letter "e" and where the absence of that letter was its central theme (he did this so successfully that an early reviewer of the book didn't notice that the entire text lacked the most frequent letter of the alphabet).[20] Other members composed poems as palindromes (that read the same backward as forward) or with each line an anagram of the one before.

One of the founding members, Raymond Queneau, constructed a book called *One Hundred Million Million Poems* (the French title is *Cent Mille Milliards de Poèmes*).[21] The book consists of ten sonnets, one on each page, printed on stiff paper with each line cut out as a separate strip. Any one line from one of the sonnets can be combined with lines from the nine other ones to form 100,000,000,000,000 different poems. The method he used of creating verses that can be split into smaller parts then recombined in many different ways, with each combination forming a coherent poem, was the same as that employed by John Peters for his versifying tables and John Clark for his Eureka machine. The Oulipo group appear not to have heard of these earlier attempts at combinatorial poetry, or if they had, they didn't acknowledge them.

The literary experiments of Oulipo chimed with avant-garde movements in the 1960s and 70s, particularly the paradoxical notion that by imposing deliberate constraints, writers become truly free. In systematically exploring what they called "potential literature" (poems or stories that might be generated by applying a particular set of constraints) the Oulipo group turned the mechanical exercises of Peters and Clark into a science of creativity. Mathematicians in the group devised complicated methods to generate stories based on the mathematics of combinatorics (counting possible ways to combine things). The poets and writers subjected themselves to rigorous constraints to produce mostly impenetrable works of literature.

Creative constraint

Constraint will become a recurring theme when, later, we meet computers as story writing machines. The key idea is that writing is necessarily constrained. By following the constraints of grammar, meaning and style, writers can create works that match a reader's sense of what is well-structured, meaningful and engaging. Constraints allow writers to control the multitude of possibilities that thought and language offer. Relax the constraints too far, and the prose or poetry becomes formless and incoherent. Impose too many constraints, and the result is stiff, pompous text. The process of forming and working within constraints is carried on below consciousness by even the youngest writer. We can't help fitting words into patterns. A good writer knows just how and when to play with the constraints on language to cause an effect on the reader.

The "Artificial Versifying" tables and the Eureka machine both worked by mechanizing the rules of Latin hexameter verse. The creative act came from their inventors, who realized that constraints can be productive. It's hard to appreciate now what a leap of imagination that was. They analyzed the rules of versifying and (in modern computer terminology) hard-coded them into a set of tables (for Peters) and a clockwork machine (for Clark) that would generate thousands of variations.

In the early 20th century, two movements, Dada and Surrealism, tried to provoke creativity by casting off constraint. Both were a reaction to the Western emphasis on logic and reason that, as they saw it, had caused the butchery of the World War and the conformity of capitalism. Dada employed satire and shock (Marcel Duchamp exhibiting a urinal as art, for example) to shake society out of complacency. One of their techniques was to create poems by cutting words out of newspapers or books, shaking them up, and putting them at random into lines. Tristan Tzara, a founder of Dada, described it in this way:[22]

TO MAKE A DADAIST POEM

Take a newspaper.
Take some scissors.
Choose from this paper an article of the length you want to make your poem.
Cut out the article.
Next carefully cut out each of the words that makes up this article and put them all in a bag.
Shake gently.
Next take out each cutting one after the other.
Copy conscientiously in the order in which they left the bag.
The poem will resemble you.
And there you are – an infinitely original author of charming sensibility, even though unappreciated by the vulgar herd.

Nowadays you don't need to go to the trouble of cutting words out of newspapers – you can have a computer do the work for you. The free Dada Poem Generator from La Salle University lets you paste text into a box, press a button and see how it jumbles into a poem.[23] We took a piece from the *Daily Mail* newspaper (about the earrings Kate Middleton wore to the Euro 2020 football final) to generate this poetic work.[24]

```
A asap they style.

Kate just.
But you;
Of collection her mappin are in and.
Out super her;
Of love so guaranteed £65 you're
be to back design colour;
```

```
We happy a if to will to the;
Has them shape set end fan webb pieces by got splash.
Click (right) likes outfit of bound
to and to hear asprey.
This sell & you'll;
Up the high add snap beaded any they're teardrop
```

In the 1950s, the writer William S. Burroughs employed a similar "cut-up method" to uncover the hidden meanings of a text. Decades later Bob Dylan, David Bowie, Kurt Cobain, and Thom Yorke of Radiohead were among the musicians who found inspiration from cutting and rearranging words.[25]

Surrealism followed Dada in experimenting with ways to activate the subconscious mind by invoking dreams and trances and by relaxing the restrictions of language. They tried automatic writing by rushing thoughts onto paper without letting language get in the way. They had many people compose a text one word at a time without seeing what the others had written, to tap the collective unconscious. The Surrealists aimed to revolutionize human experience by freeing people from false customs and restrictive structures.

The Oulipo group would have none of that. Where Surrealists opposed rational modernity by freeing the mind to explore the subconscious, the Oulipians consciously imposed constraints on poetry and prose to discover what literature might be. Where the Surrealists were overtly political, the Oulipians were determinedly academic. Where the Surrealists rejected rationality as an imposition of capitalist society, the Oulipians subverted rationality by constraining it. Each book or poem they created by imposing a new constraint was a creative work in itself and also a demonstration of the multiple possibilities offered by that constraint.

Lest that all seems too cerebral, here is a work by Elena Addomine, a distinguished member of Oplepo (the Italian equivalent of Oulipo). She wrote "homographic" poems where the same series of letters forms a poem in both Italian and English. For example, here is her poem No. 6 in Italian:[26]

Musicisti:

meno talenti ma geni
che offron tal passione a rare amanti e sacri dei.
Inganni, celate com'eran, note . . .

The same letters in the same order, after rearranging the breaks between letters, become in English:

> Music is time, not a lent image:
> niche of frontal passion,
> ear area.
> Man ties acrid ey'ing an'nice;
> latecomer, an'note.

The constraint of making the same series of letters work as a poem in Italian and in English forced Addomine to be creative, to find English phrases such as "Music is time, not" that also make sense in Italian, "Musicisti: meno t". The leftover "t" then prompted her to create a further phrase, and so on.

By the 1990s, the absurdly serious French Oulipo group, along with its offshoots in other countries, had gone out of fashion, though its founding philosophy of pataphysics continued in various forms. London, always a soft spot for eccentric movements, became home for an Institute of 'Pataphysics (the apostrophe is deliberate) which still produces a journal and engages in elaborately pretentious activities.[27] Perhaps its greatest claim to fame is that Paul McCartney of The Beatles immersed himself in the writings of Alfred Jarry.[28] The Beatles song "Maxwell's Silver Hammer" begins: "Joan was quizzical, studied pataphysical || Science in the home".

Love letters from Manchester

We come now to the birth of electronic computing. After World War 2, Alan Turing, the pioneer of digital computing, was Deputy Director of the Computing Machine Laboratory at the University of Manchester in the UK, developing an early digital computer named Manchester Mark 1.[29] At that time, there was public interest in whether these new "electronic brains" could think and create. In 1949, Turing gave an interview to *The Times* newspaper where he said, "I do not see why it [the computer] should not enter into any one of the fields normally covered by the intellect, and eventually compete on equal terms. I do not think you can even draw the line about sonnets, though the comparison is perhaps a little unfair because a sonnet written by a machine would be better appreciated by a machine."[30]

Christopher Strachey worked at the lab with Turing, and in his spare time he wrote a program to generate love letters in flowery 19th century language. Here's an example, written in the capital letters of early computer printers:

```
HONEY SWEETHEART

MY LOVEABLE INFATUATION SEDUCTIVELY WOOS YOUR
AFFECTION. YOU ARE MY BURNING LIKING: MY FOND
INFATUATION. YOU ARE MY IMPATIENT LOVE. MY DARLING
ARDOUR KEENLY PRIZES YOUR LITTLE FONDNESS.

YOURS LOVINGLY

M.U.C.
```

The sender's initials stand for Manchester University Computer. We can only speculate as to why Strachey chose to pioneer computer creativity through Victorian love letters. They are more eye-catching and amusing than, say, haiku poems (which have been favourites of later attempts at computer poetry). Also, they followed a simple algorithm:[31]

1   Open with words from two lists of salutations such as "BELOVED LOVE", "HONEY SWEETHEART".
2   Do the following 5 times:
3   Choose randomly one of two types of sentence structure: "MY (adjective) (noun) (adverb) (verb) YOUR (verb)" or "YOU ARE MY (adjective) (noun)". If two sentences of the second type follow each other, put a colon between them.
4   Fill each sentence structure with words from pre-prepared lists of adjectives, adverbs, nouns and verbs.
5   End with "YOURS (adverb)".

This algorithm is no challenge to a modern computer but was tricky to program on one from the early 1950s designed for performing mathematical operations. Over the following decades, many professional programmers and then students of computer science followed Strachey in exploring computer creativity. Initially, these attempts were to write highly constrained verse such as haiku and, later, rhyming couplets, limericks, sonnets, riddles, short stories, novels, interactive role-playing games and theatre performances. This was the birth of digital literature and computer gaming.

Computer poetry

You may be wondering whether the Oulipians employed computers to carry out their combinatorial capers. They did. In August 1961, Dimitri Starynkevitch, a computer scientist, sent Queneau examples of his *Cent Mille Milliards de Poèmes* generated by computer. Queneau wasn't pleased. The program had generated the poems at random and the Oulipo group didn't like mechanical randomness – it left no space for the reader to play and explore. They later tried ways to constrain the randomness, but, lacking interaction between reader and computer, it was all somewhat sterile. The interactions came later, in the 1980s, with personal computers.

If you studied computing in the 1980s or 90s, you probably wrote at least one program to generate language. As a doctoral student at Edinburgh University's Department of Artificial Intelligence in the late 1970s, I (Mike) went further and turned playing games with language into a PhD thesis.[32] My main work was to study how exploring language could help children develop their writing abilities. As recreation, I wrote programs to generate simple poems.

My aim was the same as the Oulipians' (though at the time I hadn't heard of them): to play with language by constraining it. At school, a friend and I had invented an imaginary language (heavily based on Latin). In my teens, I discovered generative grammars. Until then, I had only experienced grammar in red teacher's ink underlining split infinitives and dangling modifiers. Then, I came across the idea that grammar could *generate* language, not just *correct* it. That was a liberation. I found patterns in language and learned how to generate new ones. I was like a child who had been taught laboriously to read music and play tunes on the piano suddenly discovering how to improvise jazz.

I began by writing a program that simply generated words at random from a list. Then, I added the constraint of syntax. I sorted the words into parts of speech (noun, verb, adjective, adverb, etc.) and coded some patterns, such as [adverb, adverb the adjective noun verb the noun]. These produce the appearance of simple lines of poetry but make little or no sense; for example: "Proudly, slowly the sorrowful tree eats the lion". Last, I added tags to the words and patterns to show their meaning and did some clever coding to make sure the words match in meaning and have the correct word endings. Here's a demonstration of the program conversing with a human user (the human's responses are after "Request:"):

```
I will write a poem to order.
Type a request, such as: Write me a happy
poem about Christmas
```

Request: write me a happy poem about Christmas

Joy gladdens the greeting
beside the reveller revellers sing
shining the greeting rings
how the reveller sings!
sweetly Christmas sways

Request: write me some haiku

hot still petal waits
swirling snowflake flickers then
greets the hot warm sun

Request: write me a poem about hearing

Deep songs

poetry intrigues the boy
listen a soft song ends!
beside a voice a voice talks
music whispers
listen a deep voice talks!
over by a deep voice voices weep
whispering the voice weeps
fading the song fades
over by a voice voices weep
sometimes music grows
poetry troubles memory
sometimes deep voices weep
listen voices talk
eagerly young lovers whisper
beside the deep voice the voice weeps
beside the song a deep song ends
poetry threatens a desperate woman

They may have the appearance of free verse (poetry with no rhyme or metre), yet something important is missing from these and other attempts at computer poetry from that period. The verses are exercises in language generation, not expressions of lived experience. At that time, in the 1970s and 80s, just getting a metal box to produce something that looked like a poem was accomplishment enough.

Since then, a programmer has had his output published in a student poetry magazine,[33] some poets have tried to distil their imagination into code,[34] at least one book of computer poetry has been published,[35] and websites offer interactive poetry generators.[36] None of these will threaten accomplished poets, nor are they meant to. Most are exercises in programming, not poetry. But the best, from computational poets such as Nick Montfort, Alex Saum and Leo Flores, offer new poetic practices that engage readers as players of multiple games with language, art and technology.[37]

Pentametron

Perhaps the most endearing computer poetry project is Pentametron, by the conceptual artist Ranjit Bhatnagar. In 2012, he wrote a program that scans Twitter for any tweets that happen to conform to an iambic pentameter – the rhythm of Shakespeare's plays (da DUM da DUM da DUM da DUM da DUM). Then a related program matches these tweets to form sonnets, like solving a gigantic poetic jigsaw puzzle. He published the best of these as a compendium, with the title of each poem also generated by the computer.[38] Here's an example:

> **That was the worst idea of the day.**
>
> That was extremely stupid. On the real.
> why does selena gomez even try?
> I only wanna ride the ferris wheel.
> give me a bloody minute to reply!!!!
>
> I feel a separation coming on
> You think the Mississippi is in France . . .
> time for a harry potter marathon
> i wanna read a book about romance
>
> imagine being twitter famous tho
> Seen Bruno irritating ass today
> Hello hello hello hello hello
> You are a cocky asshole. Go away.
>
> Mel Gibson, legend. Lethal Weapon 4
> There's no communication anymore.

The poem brilliantly captures the frenetic opinionated emptiness of social media.[39] Each line is a slice of real human experience, distilled into Twitter. Finding tweets that scan as iambic pentameter, then juxtaposing and combining them into sonnets with the aid of a computer is, we would argue, an act of creative composition.

If computer poetry were merely a problem to be solved, then the problem would be both specious and insoluble. The technical challenges of poetry – to get lines to scan and rhyme – are easily solved with a well-crafted computer program and a big-enough store of words. The specious problem is to convince a reader that the computer-generated poem has been written by a human poet. Why bother? Poetry works as a contract between writer and reader to explore the ambiguity of language, be drawn into an extended metaphor, share an experience, evoke an emotional response. If reading a poem becomes a game of "guess which of these is written by the computer", then all the intrinsic beauty is lost and the problem is meaningless.

There is value in combining poetry and computation. John Clark built his poetry machine as a way to demonstrate the kaleidoscopic creative process. The Surrealists employed automated writing to access the subconscious mind. The Oulipians wanted to discover what literature could be. Ranjit Bhatnagar mines the internet for fragments of experience that he assembles into verse. All these have contributed to the rich field of artificial versifying. In the next chapter we explore the new territory of literature that merges human and machine creativity.

Automatic novel writers   **4**

It took just 20 years to go from a program that wrote love letters to one that created complete short stories, then a further 20 years to a published 350-page novel written in partnership with a computer.[1] Between 1973 and 1993, articles appeared in computer magazines and then in newspapers such as *The New York Times* describing in wonderment how computers were turning out stories, novels, even operas. It was a golden era for story machines. Computers were introduced into offices and homes, AI promised expert systems that would transform business and medicine, and computer storytelling programs would feed a production line to satisfy the public demand for potboiler novels. Journalists and fiction writers were fascinated and appalled. As one writer of women's fiction said with just a hint of spite: "A computer could probably do a better job than [bestselling author] Jacqueline Susann. You could program a computer to be tasteless."[2]

Then came the backlash. Of the four main attempts to program complete works of fiction during this period, two were dismissed as fakes, one was slated for producing unreadable stories, and the programmer of the fourth was threatened with a lawsuit for copying the style of the aforementioned Jacqueline Susann.

Klein's automatic novel writer

Of these early attempts to program computers to compose short stories and novels, the one with the most enduring interest was the seven-year project by Sheldon Klein and colleagues to develop an Automatic Novel Writer.

DOI: 10.4324/9781003161431-4

Sheldon Klein was professor of both computer science and linguistics at the University of Wisconsin.[3] Over his career he developed a linguistic theory of life. Starting in the early 1960s, he explored how people learn and pass on their knowledge, simulating their language skills as computer programs. Starting by writing programs to generate and combine sentences, he moved on to short stories and then to an Automatic Novel Writer.

His central idea is that each of us has a mental language system that we develop from childhood through conversation. We also have memories of the world and our actions in it, stored in our minds as a network of associations. These can be simulated on a computer.

The idea that human semantic memory is organized as interlinked concepts was already in currency, and Klein adopted this for his computer model of story generation. He added some refinements. The most important was to code a further set of rules that describe actions in the story, such as "if person X sees an affair between Y and Z, and Y is married, then X may blackmail Y". These action rules are given probabilities of occurring, so that each story the program generates is different, depending on whether an action takes place or not. An action changes the state of the story world and one event leads to another (for example, if Mary and John have an argument then the relation "friend-of" might be altered to "not-friend-of").

Murder mystery party

By the start of the 1970s, Klein and colleagues had designed and coded a substantial computer program that could generate a 2,100-word short story about a murder at a country house party. There is no doubt that the program followed the complex set of rules and networks that Klein had devised. Here's a short extract from its output, describing the murder:[4]

```
Dr. Bartholomew Hume blackmailed Edward. Edward was afraid
of Dr. Hume. Lord Edward decided to kill Dr. Batholomew
Hume. The day was Sunday. The time was sunrise. Lord
Edward got up. Lord Edward went to the dark corridor. Lord
Edward hid. Edward had a candle holder. Dr. Bartholomew
awakened early. Dr. Bartholomew was usually early. Dr.
Hume went for the walk. Edward waited for Hume. Lord
Edward surprised Hume. Edward hit Dr. Bartholomew Hume
with the candle holder. Dr. Bartholomew Hume groaned
weakly. Dr. Hume died. Edward returned to the bedroom.
```

In another run of the program, the murder might unfold differently, for example with James, the house owner, being poisoned by the butler.

Klein's murder mystery generator was an impressive advance in story generation. His program not only composed a complete short story, it also told the story in well-formed English sentences. The program set up a story world of a house party. It added characters and developed their traits, such as greed, jealousy and anger. It devised a sex scene that motivated one character to commit blackmail and another to take revenge. It described in some detail the murder and its detection. It kept track of events over time so that, for example, once they discovered the murder, the characters didn't go off and play a game of croquet.

Not content with this success, Klein over-sold the program and its contribution to linguistics. At an international conference in 1973, in a paper with the title "Automatic Novel Writing: A Status Report" he made the astonishing claim that "The novel writer described herein is part of an automated linguistic tool so powerful and of such methodological significance that we are compelled to claim a major breakthrough in linguistic and computational linguistic research." His system, Klein claimed, could model human language and social behaviour as it evolved over time. Furthermore, it was supposedly based on a computational model of language that trumped contemporary theories of linguistics and psychology.

The yawning gap between Klein's rhetoric of modelling society through computational linguistics and the reality of a murder mystery story about croquet and candle holders was clear from the start. Other researchers unkindly pointed out that the Automatic Novel Writer could only write minor variations on the same story.[5] The order of events was fixed, the characters and location were set in advance, and the murder wasn't even a mystery to the reader, since midway through the story the killer, victim and weapon were revealed. After describing how the murder was committed, each version of the story tells how the remaining characters gather and call an incompetent detective. Then one of the house guests finds a clue and solves the crime.

Klein seemed unconcerned about the banality of the stories produced by his Automatic Novel Writer. He knew that his system was powerful and innovative, so he didn't need to prove that by making it write anything more spectacular. When researcher Ed Kahn raised the issue that the program revealed the murderer in the middle of the story, Klein responded:

> Kahn is right in saying that, in this particular detective story model, the true detective function is absent. This defect is an artifact of the

need to construct an example quickly in time for a conference presentation, and in time for my immediately subsequent visit to Moscow on an exchange program.[6]

It wrote detective stories that lacked detection.

That problem might have been fixed by omitting the description of the murder in the middle of the story, giving one member of the cast extra information about the motives of other characters and a way of finding clues, then revealing details of the murder at the end of the story. Klein's linguistic system was powerful enough to do that. It was able to model the private knowledge of each character in a story. It assigned each character a separate memory network and set of language rules. It could give one character better powers of deduction or simulate an argument between two people holding different knowledge or beliefs. However, these functions were never added to the working system. The result is that Klein advanced the science of machine storytelling through his semantic grammars, but the program's outputs didn't entertain as fiction.

What's missing?

A deeper issue is that Klein's language rules and memory networks aren't entirely up to the task of creating varied language and satisfying stories. His program can generate well-formed sentences such as: "Mary greets the small man", "John owns a big bicycle". It can call on its memory network to make sure that a tall man owns a big (not small) bicycle. But English language has subtleties that need further rules to be captured. For example, "small woman", "tall woman" and "small bicycle" are all acceptable phrases, but the phrase "tall bicycle" is not normal English. If the sentences were part of a story, we might want to know where they are riding their bicycles to and why they are cycling, not driving cars. If the man in the story greets the woman, does it follow that the woman should greet the man?

A human author of a story that contains the two sentences "John is riding a small bicycle. He greets Mary." might be including cycling as a metaphor for freedom or to emphasize John's height or as a way to show that John is healthy. Each of these would need further rules and extended networks. That's just for a couple of sentences about people and their bicycles. To generate a series of intriguing murder mysteries from first principles would take years of work in building rules and networks.

Sheldon Klein had neither time nor inclination to stick with a murder in a country house.

With his student researchers, Klein went on to design a program that composed the words and music for an opera, *Revolt in Flatland*.[7] He explored how computers could model the processes of human reflection (through rules for behaviour that inspect and change other rules), dreaming (by transferring a conflict to a fantasy world) and social interaction (by building simulated beings who converse by acting out and exchanging their rules of language and behaviour). A few years before his death in 2005, Sheldon Klein wrote a paper exploring human creativity from the Stone Age to the present day and into the future.[8] An account of creativity based on language alone, he said, will never capture the ambiguity and complexity of human cognition. What's required is a way to model *systems* of knowledge and behaviour. These systems need to account for diverse activities such as architecture, music and language. They should be hierarchies, with each layer summarizing and describing the layer below. And they should be dynamic, to capture changes in belief and society over short and long periods of time.

Unfortunately, Klein's legacy in automated story writing is not his grand theory of human creativity; rather, it is a set of barely readable murder mysteries. It's a lesson to academics and companies working on AI – they will be judged in the long run by their products, not their claims.

The Policeman's Beard Is Half Constructed

The other book projects during the 1980s and 90s didn't have Klein's academic clout. They are noteworthy because each resulted in a published book that sparked controversy.

The most engaging and readable of these books was *The Policeman's Beard Is Half Constructed*.[9] In the introduction, William Chamberlain and Thomas Etter claim that "with the exception of this introduction, the writing of this book was all done by computer". The published book is a compilation of dialogues between human users and a computer, accompanied by quaint pictures in the style of 19th century illustrations. The computer program, named Racter, ran on a Z80 microcomputer, a hobbyist desktop machine of the early 1980s.[10] Programming such a tiny computer to generate a book was, to put it mildly, a challenge.

Chamberlain and Etter wrote a programming language, INRAC, to generate texts and converse with users of the program. They sold INRAC and Racter, along with an interactive tutorial, for $244.96, a hefty price in 1985.

Racter was what would nowadays be called a chatbot. It held a surreal conversation with the user. Here's an extract from a typical dialogue, with the words after the ">" symbol typed by the user:

```
> Can you write a novel?

  I can. Would you like to hear a story?

> Yes please

  Who should the story be about?

> Charlotte

  Drinking wine is Charlotte's desire. Swallowing steak
  is Charlotte's passion. Nevertheless Benton sees only
  tomatoes. This is peculiar! Charlotte croons to Benton
  about wine and steak yet Benton will glimpse tomatoes. This
  is peculiar. Benton skipped to Charlotte's blue home and
  began to embarrass and incite Charlotte while Charlotte
  was singing about steak. Simmer down. By reason of the
  fact that Benton's own blue cottage was scary; he whispered
  nervously to Charlotte "Do you follow me?" This slaughtered
  Charlotte. Meanwhile a scientist began to munch some
  cucumbers. Benton was angry. Suddenly he knew that to spy a
  spinach is not to glimpse it. Charlotte realises that wine
  and steak are not tomatoes. The scientist does not. Are you
  interested? Benton is infuriated and weary, nevertheless
  some cucumbers would allow him to be worried during the time
  that Charlotte assassinated the scientist. If "I can write
  a novel" occurred to a poet, he would be a clever poet.
  If it's not too personal a question do you have a soul?

> I think I have a soul

  You think you have a soul? What does it mean to have a
  soul? Maybe this will explain: Once Bill Chamberlain
  was discussing dirtiness with a centipede. Homer
  came along and said "Bill Chamberlain, your soul is
  just an amusement of your body." Next question.

> What is the meaning of life?

  I don't know what is the meaning of life. Apple probably
  wouldn't like Adam. Is having a soul contagious?
```

We know that this is a genuine output from the program, because the commercial version of Racter is now available to run online, for free, in a web browser.[11] From our interactions with the program and reports by computer scientists who inspected its code, it's clear that the program works like the classic party game of Mad Libs.[12] It has templates for sentences, with gaps to be filled in from lists of stored words in various categories, for example:

> By reason of the fact that <name>'s own <colour> <object> was scary; he whispered nervously to <character> "<speech>".

When it runs, the program fills each part of the template inside the < > brackets with a word from its relevant list. The word for <character> is provided at the start by the user. So, if the user gives Hilda as the name of the main character, the foregoing template might generate from its organized store of words:

> By reason of the fact that Archie's own pink hair dryer was scary; he whispered nervously to Hilda "Do you not agree?"

Chamberlain and Etter programmed some clever additional features to keep a sense of continuity and style. For example, the dialogue at the end keeps a focus on the word "soul" across a series of questions and answers.

The quality of Racter's output depends entirely on the ingenuity of its programmers in writing quirky templates and amusing words, with sufficient variety in these to keep a story going without it becoming either boring or too nonsensical. Chamberlain and Etter got the balance about right.

So far, so playful. However, some pages contain longer pieces of prose, with four characters and their quirks forming bizarre short stories. The versions of the Racter program sold to the public were incapable of generating the stories printed in the book.

Nothing incites writers more than literary fakery. Commentators have condemned *The Policeman's Beard Is Half Constructed* as a hoax[13] and its program Racter of being a parlour trick[14] for text "degeneration" rather than generation.[15] One review offered a litany of criticisms: the book is an egotistical mishmash of incomprehensible ramblings, its Racter program is rigid, the programming language is poorly designed, Chamberlain and Etter weren't academics and couldn't, or wouldn't, explain their work.[16] More favourable reviews have described *The Policeman's Beard* as the first cyber-novel, a meld of human and machine creativity. None of the critics seemed to have grasped two points. *The Policeman's Beard* was a bit of anarchic techno-literary fun, and the over-expensive commercial version of Racter was cut down to fit onto home microcomputers with limited computer memory, which is why it couldn't generate longer and more complex stories.

Bagabone, Hem 'I Die Now

Almost everything about *Bagabone, Hem 'I Die Now* is a genuine mystery. The book exists and was published in 1980 by Vantage Press, a self-publishing company based in the United States – that much we know.[17] On the front cover, below a drawing of a woman sitting beside a lake in what looks like a tropical paradise, are the words "by Melpomene".[18] A brief description on the back of the dust jacket explains that Melpomene is a computer programmed by experts in literature, linguistics and computers at the Institute of Science and Technology, Jagiellonian University, Krakow Poland.

According to the book cover, the language experts took English verb patterns and semantic (i.e. meaning) units drawn from 20th-century women writers, as well as D. H. Lawrence, James Joyce, and some "angry young men" of the 1960s. They added elements of Pidgin English and French, to produce *Bagabone, Hem 'I Die Now*. Melpomene, according to the blurb, picked the title which, translated from Pidgin English, means, "Bagabone (a character in the novel) is dying".

Little of this appears to match reality. There is a Jagiellonian University in Krakow, Poland, but there is no evidence that it once had an Institute of Science and Technology. The copyright holder of the book is an Englishman, G. E. Hughes. The *Computerworld* magazine published an article on *Bagabone* in 1980.[19] The magazine interviewed two experts in linguistics and AI who pronounced that no computer could have created what was claimed for Melpomene. *Computerworld* also contacted a representative of the publisher, who repeated what was on the book cover, but was unable to reach G. E. Hughes. To add to the mystery, a book published in 1984 on computers and creativity authored by Donald Michie, a British pioneer of computing, mentions *Bagabone* in terms that suggest Michie knew its creator, G. E. Hughes. According to Michie, Hughes and some colleagues at the Jagiellonian University of Cracow (sic) programmed the computer to produce a complete short novel as a "giant game of Consequences".[20] That suggests the plot for the book might have been assisted by a computer program, with the machine proposing characters and actions for each episode.

What of the book itself? A photographic scan of the entire book is available to read online so you can judge for yourself whether it was written by human, computer, or a combination of both.[21]

Here are the opening lines of the book:

> Margery Hariman looked at herself in the full-length mirror of her dressing table in the main bedroom of The Rise, Jansoon Crescent, Suviara, and sighed. Suviara is the capital of the Talisman Islands, an archipelago in the South Pacific, east of New Guinea, and through the louver windows the mirror reflected the lights of the main island, Santabala. She was not interested in the lights of Suviara Bay; only in the curves of her own reflection. She saw a well-proportioned body; lovely, soft, round limbs; a slender waist; and firm, slightly pendulous breasts; a graceful, golden athletic figure, with elegant legs and intelligent ankles.

Enough! The combination of purple prose, over-complex plot and knowledge of ex-pat life all suggest a hoax by a human author, perhaps designed to boost sales of the self-published novel.

Just This Once

The fourth computer-generated novel ought to have been the most noteworthy.[22] Scott French was an electronic surveillance consultant and self-taught computer programmer. His eight-year project began as a bet with friends that a computer could write a novel. A year later, with no novel and $300 poorer, he had become obsessed with the challenge.[23] He learned programming, spent $50,000 on the latest Macintosh computer and commercial AI software, and in 1993 *Just This Once* was published with a first printing of 15,000 hardcover copies.

There is no doubt that the book was a collaboration between man and machine. As French said in an interview with *The New York Times*, "If I'd written it myself, this book would have been done seven or eight years ago".[24] French took apart Jacqueline Susann's novel *The Valley of the Dolls* and coded its structure as "if . . . then" rules that indicated how a character would react to a situation, how a particular setting would advance the plot, and how Susann would describe the actions in words. Having written several hundred of these rules for style and structure, French held a dialogue with his program. As French describes it, the computer posed questions, French would respond, and the computer would produce the story a few sentences at a time. For example, the computer might ask French to indicate the "cattiness factor" in a scene on a scale of 1 to 10. If French responded with 8, the computer would craft a sentence where the characters "screamed" and "shrieked" at each other. French estimated that he wrote 10% of *Just This Once* unedited by the computer and his program wrote 25%.[25] The remaining two thirds was a partnership between man and computer.

The book received mixed reviews. Most commented that it successfully mimicked the style of a trashy novel about money, sleaze, and tragedy. Some, such as *Publishers Weekly*, noted that the book would have been entirely unremarkable save for the fact that it was written with the aid of a computer.[26] To Scott French, that was the point of the eight-year exercise. He had succeeded in deconstructing a formulaic novel, defining its language and structure as rules for an AI program, and generating a new potboiler novel in the same style.

A testament to success was that the estate of Jacqueline Susann reportedly threated to sue Scott French for copying her style. They settled out of court for half of French's profits, with the estate controlling publicity for the book.[27]

By far the most complete computer-generated novel, *Just This Once* is also the least controversial. Scott French never claimed that his program had crafted the entire book. He beavered away at learning programming and coding the rules of style for a formulaic novel. The resulting novel was in the style of Jaqueline Susann but sufficiently different to be a tribute, not a copy. Of all four attempts at computer-generated novels in the 1980s, French's project is the best demonstration of how story machines and writers might work together in the future. It deserves to be celebrated as the first equal collaboration between human and machine in writing a complete novel-length story.

A word of caution is need here. Capturing the style of one author as a set of generative rules took eight years of work. French undoubtedly spent a good proportion of this time in learning to program and he had to fit the project around his full-time job. Nevertheless, describing an author's style as formal rules and structures that can be interpreted by a computer is currently a painstaking process. Can it be speeded up? That's a question for later in this book.

NaNoGenMo

There have been attempts since the 1990s to generate novel-length works of fiction, but none with the panache and impact of the quartet discussed in this chapter.[28] The most enterprising generator of novels is David Cope, Professor Emeritus at the University of California. Of over 100 books published in his name, ten have been generated by ALMA (Artificial Linguistic Machine Algorithm), a program he wrote to mimic human creativity.[29]

In 2013, the computer scientist and artist Darius Kazemi proposed an event each November for entrants to write computer code within one month that generates a 50,000-word novel.[30] National Novel Generation Month (NaNoGenMo) has run each year since then. NaNoGenMo has inspired scores of computer scientists and media students to try their skills at generating a novel and then share the computer code and output. As you might expect from a month of work, the results are sometimes imaginative but rarely inspiring.

A standout from the NaNoGenMo exercise in creative coding is *The Annals of the Parrigues*, a beautifully-crafted guide to an imagined ancient English kingdom.[31] It was developed by Emily Short as a journey of discovery by human and computer. When Short moved to the UK in 2015 she became fascinated by the names of English towns and villages. She wrote a program to generate imaginary English placenames, such as Shadwicke, Lost Drincham and Brooknesford. This led her to realize that names indicated something about the town (for example, "ford" equals "river crossing"). She designed a series of programs to enrich and explore her imagined land, based on five elemental themes: salt, beeswax, venom, mushroom and egg. Each theme suggested a vocabulary and a way of writing: salt indicated dryness, law, solitude, exactness; mushroom stood for growth, fertility, repetition and so on.

Equipped with the five basic themes and a grammar to generate descriptions of towns and their inhabitants, Short set about compiling the guidebook. She describes this as a genuine collaboration with the machine. Short generated guides to a few towns and provinces, then wrote some footnotes herself. She refined and extended the program, writing new content inspired by the text produced so far. Towards the end of the project, she began to interfere with the text, adding her own alluring prose. The result is a whimsical guide to a kingdom that ought to have been. Here's part of the entry for Tweedmore:

Tweedmore   *Dank Streets – Gloomy Afternoons*

The name of Tweedmore appears first in a cycle of short poems nine centuries old. The text runs to five volumes, and purchasers at Esteney Sisters will be given a complimentary case in which to carry it away.

The town is built at one end of a large and ancient forest. The streets are cramped and narrow, especially in the older parts of the town.

Excursions The most beautiful prospect of Tweedmore is that afforded by looking over one's shoulder on departure.

Lodging Those accustomed to a door that locks may find themselves disappointed in Tweedmore, which affords only a tiny thatched building under the name of FENUGREEK AND SPONGE. We were once served slug meat that was $\frac{156}{164}$ gristle.

Transportation It is advisable to change horses at THE PIGEON INN. It is a shabby building thanks to the poverty of the town.

Nick Montfort, poet and Professor of Digital Media at the Massachusetts Institute of Technology (MIT), is a mainstay of NaNoGenMo. He specializes in coding small programs to generate big works. For the 2017 event he produced a computer-generated novel, *Hard West Turn*, about gun violence in the United States. His program (270 lines of code) searches Wikipedia for accounts of recent shootings and assembles fragments of these into an evocative textual collage. Montfort founded the Using Electricity series for computer-generated works.[32]

Approaches to story generation

The attempts at writing a novel by computer nicely illustrate different approaches to story generation. Klein's Automatic Novel Writer represents the *language* method. This involves the programmer analyzing the structures of human language and coding these as rules to generate text, constrained by a network of associated meanings. Further software procedures model the flow of events from one episode to the next.

The Racter program behind *The Policeman's Beard Is Half Constructed* is an example of the *dialogue* method. The program holds a conversation with a human user and builds on this dialogue to form a coherent story. At each turn, one or more inbuilt templates match the pattern of words typed by the user and construct a plausible response. This method is at the heart of some interactive computer games, leading to new ways of combining games and computer-generated stories.

Just This Once embodies the *expert system* method, where the writing style of one or more authors is coded as a set of rules to generate a flow of text in that style.

The Annals of the Parrigues nicely demonstrates how a creative coder can build a *storyworld* in a machine and express it through language that is partly controlled by the program, yet often surprises its designer.

In the next chapter we see how Klein and others built on foundations from the scientific study of language to design programs that would tell not just one story but a set of folk tales.

The shape of a story   **5**

We come now to the engines that drive story machines. For the Eureka, its engine was a clockwork mechanism of weight, cables, pulleys and cogwheels. For computer story genereators, the engine is computational method: a story grammar, neural network, Markov chain, production rules, or others. In this and the next chapter we'll look in more depth at two of these – story grammars and neural networks – because they illustrate contrasting ways to devise a creative language machine. The first models the structure of language, the second simulates part of the human brain.

A revolution in the study of language

We left Sheldon Klein and his team of linguists in the previous chapter claiming that their computer program to generate versions of a story about murder in a country house was a "major breakthrough in linguistic and computational linguistic research".[1] Clearly, Klein could see something that his critics couldn't. That something was the power of computational grammars to generate not just one type of story but many. To do so would mean analyzing how stories are structured, then extending the program to produce not just variations on a single story but distinctly new stories.

The foundations for a formal analysis of stories were laid 70 years earlier in the unlikely context of the Russian revolution. Viktor Borisovich Shlovsky was born in 1893 in St Petersburg, a vibrant city of intellectual and cultural sophistication.[2] The factories surrounding the city were breeding grounds for revolution. Shlovsky studied at St Petersburg University then joined the

DOI: 10.4324/9781003161431-5

army as a driving instructor for armoured cars in the city. There, in the midst of the World War 1, he founded Opoyaz, an acronym that translates from Russian as the Society for the Study of Poetic Language.[3]

The name looks similar to Oulipo, the group of experimental writers we met in Chapter 2. Like Oulipo, Opoyaz comprised a group of mainly male intellectuals, writers and poets. Influenced by the Futurist movement, they saw literature as a machine for turning the raw material of language into complex works.[4] They proposed to study language in the same way a scientist might investigate the properties of a material such as steel. Unlike Oulipo, the men of Opoyaz didn't gather in country houses to drink cognac and play word games.[5] They met in the kitchen of an abandoned St Petersburg apartment and were soon thrown into the turmoil of the Russian revolution.

Shlovsky took part in the February revolution of 1917, was wounded fighting against the German army on the Southeastern Front, returned to St Petersburg, was posted to Persia, where he fought off Cossack troops, returned again to his home city in 1918 and took part in a failed plot to over-throw the Bolshevik government, went into hiding in Russia and the Ukraine, and was eventually pardoned due to his connections with the novelist Maxim Gorky. His two brothers were executed by the Soviet regime and his sister died of hunger in St Petersburg in 1919. Shlovsky's further adventures took him into the Red Army, to Finland and then to Berlin. High spirited to the end of his life, Shlovsky died in Moscow in 1984.

The lasting contribution of Opoyaz and others in the Russian Formalist movement was the scientific study of literature. Shklovsky proposed that a writer of literary language should take the familiar and make it feel strange to the reader.[6] This connects with the point made in Chapter 2 that good writing can be deliberately unsettling. He also set out an important distinction between the underlying sequence of events in a story (the "fabula") and how that story is told (the "syuzhet", or plot).[7] A creative writer will employ devices such as digressions, flashbacks, and revealing of future events to make the linear story mysterious or challenging to a reader. (A major failing of Klein's murder program was that it had no way to plot a good story. It just generated a murder mystery as a sequence of events, revealing who committed the murder in the middle of the tale).

Another native of St Petersburg, Vladimir Propp, took the scientific study of language a step further.[8] Compared to Shlovsky, Propp led a sedate life as an academic, studying Russian folk tales as a botanist might study plants to discover their underlying form (or morphology). In 1928 he published *Morphology of the Folktale*.[9]

Russian fairy stories and Harry Potter

For *Morphology of the Folktale*, Propp analyzed 100 traditional Russian fairy tales. He found that while the characters and their names change from one tale to the next, the actions these characters perform are similar. For example, in different tales:

1   A tsar gives an eagle to a hero. The eagle carries the hero away to another kingdom.
2   An old man gives Sucenko a horse. The horse carries Sucenko away to another kingdom.
3   A sorcerer gives Ivan a little boat. The boat takes Ivan to another kingdom.
4   A princess gives Ivan a ring. Young men appearing from out of the ring carry Ivan away to another kingdom.

And so on. Each of these short extracts from the folk tales has the same form: a character gives a magical object to the hero, and the object carries the hero to another place.

Then Propp meticulously labelled each of the actions undertaken by a story character (which he called "functions") and described how one function follows another in the story, such as (later in a story):

XVI. THE HERO AND VILLIAN JOIN IN DIRECT COMBAT (*struggle*. Designation H.)
XVII. THE HERO IS BRANDED (*branding, marking*. Designation J.)
XVIII. THE VILLIAN IS DEFEATED (*victory*. Designation I.)

The 31 basic actions by characters in a fairy tale could be arranged in different ways like ingredients in a recipe. No tale included all 31, but most tales involved an initial lack (such as a princess being abducted), the hero leaving home, being challenged on the journey, receiving a magical agent (such as a ring) to help in the quest, confronting and defeating the villain, returning home with a prize, and getting a reward (often, marrying the princess). In some stories, more than one person sets out on the quest. Sometimes the returning hero isn't recognized and faces further challenges. But a Russian fairy tale normally ends happily with the hero being rewarded.

Alongside the 31 functions, Propp listed seven types of characters that feature in the tales:

1   Villain – an evil character who creates struggles for the hero.
2   Dispatcher – who sets the hero on his quest (e.g., the father of the princess).

3 Helper – some magical being who helps the hero on his journey.
4 Princess – the person who the hero deserves but can't initially marry due to some injustice.
5 Donor – a character who gives the hero a magical object, perhaps after a test.
6 Hero – who reacts to the Dispatcher, goes on a journey, gets a magical object, defeats the villain and weds the princess.
7 False hero – someone who takes the credit for the hero's successes.

These character types will look familiar to anyone who has read the Harry Potter books. Throughout the seven books, the hero Harry Potter struggles against the villain Voldemort, who killed his parents. A letter from Hogwarts delivered by dispatcher Hagrid sets Harry off on his quest. He is helped by a whole array of magical beings, including Ron and Hermione. The kindly headmaster of Hogwarts, Albus Dumbledore, donates to Harry Potter a magical object, the Cloak of Invisibility. Harry the hero goes on many journeys and, in the Battle of Hogwarts, repels Voldemort's curse, killing him. An epilogue to the books describes Harry as happily married to Ginny, with Ron married to Hermione. And anyone who has read the books will be able to list false self-proclaimed heroes.

This is not to say J. K. Rowling had read *Morphology of the Folktale* and modelled the Harry Potter books on its character types and plot structures.[10] Rather, she was steeped in British folklore and mythology, which over centuries has imbibed folk tale structures and characters from many countries. That's why people see similarities among Harry Potter, Lord of the Rings and Roald Dahl's stories. The authors all drew on the common stock of fairy tales yet reworked them in new and magical ways.

Formulas for folk tales

In 1958, thirty years after it was first published in Russia, *Morphology of the Folktale* was translated into English. It was an immediate success among the new breed of structural linguists in Europe and the USA. Propp's work influenced European structuralists such as Claude Lévi-Strauss and Roland Barthes. Lévi-Strauss had earlier proposed a formula for the structure of narratives, but that was based on oppositions (such as "east versus west", "upper world versus lower world").[11] He and Propp conducted a brief literary spat. Lévi-Strauss praised Propp for his innovation, then criticized him for studying fairy tales, not myths, and rejected Propp's analysis of the sequence of story events as obvious and superficial. Propp struck back, claiming his analysis was based on a rigorous study of the data, whereas

Lévi-Strauss was conjuring up oppositions in his own mind. In a perceptive commentary on the debate between Propp and Lévi-Strauss, the folklorist Alan Dundes notes that the two were talking past each other. Propp was formalizing the language structure of folk tales, whereas Lévi-Strauss was analyzing the inherent meaning of myths.[12]

In addition to inspiring structural analysis of narratives, Propp also offered a scientific method to generate stories. In an appendix to his book, Propp lists the order of events for each of the 100 fairy stories, with each letter or symbol standing for one story function (such as A for "villainy" and ↑ for "departure of the hero from home"). His story sequences look like highly compressed computer programs, for example:

$$ABC \uparrow FH - IK \downarrow LM - NQ \, Ex \, UW^*$$

Propp realized that not only did these formulas describe the structure of Russian fairytales, but the elements could be combined in different ways to generate new ones. He wrote, "It is possible to artificially create new plots of an unlimited number" by starting with function A (the villain causes harm to a family or community) and moving in sequence through the story actions, leaving out some and repeating others until the happy ending (function W) is reached.[13] Although he didn't have access to a computer in the 1920s, Propp sowed the seeds of artificial story generation by proposing a computational mechanism to generate story plots.

We were tempted to end this section by drawing parallels between the Russian formalists of Opoyaz, exploring the structures that governed literature, and attempts by the Soviet Union to compel writers and artists to glorify communist values. But Shklovsky fought throughout his life against the dogma of Soviet realism. He saw the work of Opoyaz as being to understand the constraints on literature and art and then squash them, to make the familiar strange, so we might see the world in its glory and cruelty.

The computer tales of Joseph Grimes

Morphology of the Folktale was published in English at the just same time as the first experiments with computer generation of text. A pioneer was Joseph E. Grimes.[14] Grimes studied for a PhD in Linguistics at Cornell University. On moving to Mexico City, he became fascinated with automating the structure of folk tales. In 1960–1961 he programmed an IBM computer at the

Universidad Nacional Autónoma de México to generate stories. It worked by moving from episode to episode, choosing the next element at random, but keeping track of the characters. Here is the only surviving example of the earliest recorded attempt to create complete stories by computer:

```
A lion has been in trouble for a long time. A dog
steals something that belongs to the lion. The hero,
lion, kills the villain, dog, without a fight. The
hero, lion, thus is able to get his possession back.
```

The story generated by Grimes' program is highly compressed, but it has the very basic components of a Propp story structure. The hero lacks something and determines to get it back. The hero kills the villain. The hero is rewarded.

This was not just an exercise in computer programming. As a linguist, Grimes was interested in whether people from different cultures shared the same basic structure of a fairy story. He showed translations of his stories to people from indigenous communities in Mexico to see how they recognized the story structure as part of their culture. Grimes even had plans to publish a set of computer-generated folk tales as a resource for linguists, but it never came to fruition. The stories produced by his program had Propp's elements in miniature but were too short to be of use for research into storytelling. Nevertheless, Grimes has his place in the annals of story machines as programmer of the first automated storyteller.

Fifty folk tales by computer

The first attempt to cast Propp's formulas in full into a computer program came from who else but Sheldon Klein and his team. Realizing the limitations of their earlier murder mystery program, but convinced of the power of their linguistic methods, in 1974 they set about converting not only Propp's formulas but also the myth structures of Lévi-Strauss into computer code. The aim was to show how their linguistic methods could be a basis for describing human language and behaviour.

They coded Propp's story sequences as data for a computer program that combined them according to rules and constraints laid out in *Morphology of the Folktale*. Some story elements could be left out, other elements could be repeated. The program then added the names of characters and objects and rendered it in English sentences to make a complete and consistent story.

A paper by Klein and colleagues lists 50 short folk tales generated by their program.[15] Here is one of them:

> The Morevnas live in a certain kingdom. The father is
> Aliosha. Katrina is the only child. Marco also lives in
> the same land. Vladimir is Marco's child. A dragon appears
> in the certain kingdom. The dragon imprisons Vladimir.
> Marco calls for help from Aliosha. Aliosha decides to
> search for Vladimir. Aliosha leaves on a search.
>
> Aliosha meets a bull along the way. The bull brawls in
> a forest with Aliosha. The bull twice repels Aliosha.
> They fight for the third time. Aliosha defeats the bull.
> A magic sword, a magic steed and a magic bird are given
> to Aliosha. Aliosha travels to the location of Vladimir
> in the other kingdom. Aliosha travels on the magic steed.
> Aliosha finds the dragon. They fight in an open field.
> Aliosha defeats the dragon with the aid of the magic
> sword. Vladimir is obtained by Aliosha. Aliosha starts
> back home. The dragon flys [sic] after Aliosha. Aliosha
> escapes by flying on the magic bird. Aliosha returns home.

There are some weaknesses in the telling – Katrina is introduced but doesn't feature in the action; it isn't clear why Marco should ask Aliosha to retrieve his son rather than embarking on the quest himself; the tale has no grand finale – but these are minor problems. The characters are consistent and Aliosha employs all three magic objects (sword, steed and bird) to defeat the dragon. The story makes sense and looks like a folk tale.

Klein had found a means to express Propp's fairy tale structures in forms that a computer could interpret and turn into prose. Could a similar method generate other types of story, such as an epic, a mystery or a romance? What's needed is a general mechanism to generate story structures.

Story grammars

The renowned linguist and philosopher George Lakoff proposed the method of story grammars as a way to link modern generative grammars with Propp's story structures when he was a young graduate student in the early 1970s.[16] The idea behind story grammars is simple yet powerful: take a formalism that can generate sentences and apply it to stories.

The linguist Noam Chomsky had already shown in the late 1950s that language rules can describe how people create and understand sentences. Klein realized that the same structures can not only generate sentences about our everyday world but also about fantasy worlds of stories. He was fascinated by the power of a small set of rules to evoke scenes and actions. To give a basic example, the rules to produce simple sentences are:

1   SENTENCE -> NOUN-PHRASE VERB-PHRASE
2   NOUN-PHRASE -> determiner noun
3   NOUN-PHRASE -> determiner adjective noun
4   NOUN-PHRASE -> name
5   VERB-PHRASE -> verb NOUN-PHRASE

These five rules can generate innumerable well-formed sentences. Start with Rule 1. It says to replace a SENTENCE with a NOUN-PHRASE followed by a VERB-PHRASE.

Rules 2 to 4 show different ways to replace NOUN-PHRASE. Let's choose one at random, Rule 3, and generate:

determiner adjective noun VERB-PHRASE (Rule 3)

Then we call on Rule 5, replacing VERB-PHRASE to get:

determiner adjective noun verb NOUN-PHRASE (Rule 5)

Again, we choose at random from Rules 2 to 4 to replace NOUN-PHRASE:

determiner adjective noun verb determiner noun (Rule 2)

Now we have a series of parts of speech that can't be expanded further. Last, we look up a table of words such as the one below:

noun	man, woman, dog, bird
verb	saw, ate, owned, liked
adjective	tall, old, small, big, little
determiner	the, a
name	John, Mary

and choose one word at random for each part of speech, for example:

the old woman saw a bird

Each route through the grammar rules generates a different sentence. Code the rules as a computer program, add rules for more complex sentences and some further code to select words that match for meaning, and you have a basic language generator.

The idea behind story grammars is to take the rules up a level, so that instead of producing sentences, they output story structures. A story grammar shows how a story can be split into parts:

STORY -> initial-situation + ACTIVE-EVENT + final-situation

This says that a simple story consists of an initial situation, an active event and a final situation (or beginning, middle and end). The endpoints of a story grammar aren't words, but individual situations or actions by characters in the story (what Propp called "functions", such as "the villain is defeated").

Just as a sentence grammar can be called on either to describe the structure of a sentence or to compose a new one, so a story grammar can be used to analyze the structure of stories or generate new tales. Below is a story grammar for French medieval epics created by Lyn Pemberton.[17] Pemberton studied for a PhD at the University of Toronto on the story structure of French epic poetry, then went the University of Sussex where she designed a model for generating epics by computer, which she called Gester.

1 STORY -> initial-situation + ACTIVE-EVENT + final-situation
2 ACTIVE-EVENT -> COMPLICATION + ACTION-SEQUENCE
3 COMPLICATION -> motivating-motif* + motivation
4 ACTION-SEQUENCE -> PLAN + QUALIFICATION + ACTION + resolution
5 ACTION -> action* + STORY + ACTION | action*
6 PLAN -> informing-act* + plan-proper
7 QUALIFICATION -> qualifying-act* + qualification-proper

The Gester story grammar generates stories that start with an initial situation where the main character lacks an object (for a medieval epic, this would be something grand, such as "Charles lacked a city"). Then follows the active event at the heart of the story, where the character (or a surrogate) tries to gain the object. The story ends with a final situation where the character succeeds in his quest.

Each item in capital letters can be unpacked by one of the grammar rules into further items. So, the second rule says that an ACTIVE-EVENT can be split into a COMPLICATION followed by an ACTION-SEQUENCE. Each of these, in turn, can become a further sequence of items by following the direction of the story grammar.

For the previous Gester grammar, starting with STORY, the rules unpack in the following way:

STORY

initial-situation + ACTIVE-EVENT + final-situation (Rule 1)

initial-situation + COMPLICATION + ACTION-SEQUENCE + final-situation (Rule 2)

initial-situation + motivating-motif* + motivation + ACTION-SEQUENCE + final-situation (Rule 3)

and so on.

An item in lower case is an end-item (or "terminal"). It isn't expanded by the rules but needs to be fleshed out with text. An "initial-situation" for a French medieval epic could be "Charles lacked a city" or "Bertrand longed for a castle". Pemberton's Gester program fills out each terminal with pre-written prose to move the story forward.

A star (*) after an item means it can be repeated (for example, a story can have multiple motivating motifs). A bar (|) means "or". Thus, Rule 5 can be unpacked as follows: an ACTION story element can be one or more "action" sequences of text, followed by a STORY element, followed by an ACTION element. Or it could be one or more basic actions. This rule shows how a full story can be embedded within another story. This, combined with repeating story elements, gives the set of rules the power to produce complex stories, with one tale inside another.

Pemberton programmed Gester with devices to create a coherent story, such as linking together the parts of the story, creating a consistent set of characters, leaving out actions that aren't relevant, and weaving together elements from the main story with the one embedded within it. Here is a story from Gester. It starts with the French King Charles seeking a city to invade. He wins the city of Narbonne, where he sees Blancheflor and determines to gain her as a wife. He then forgets to reward his companion and throws his enemy into prison. The story then returns to his desire for a wife.

```
Charles lacked a city. As a result of hearing of Narbonne
Charles wanted Narbonne. Then Aymeri agreed to help
Charles. Then Charles and Aymeri rode to Narbonne.
Then, Charles attacked the walls of Narbonne, currently
```

controlled by Baufumez, helped by Aymeri. Thibaut and
Clarion threw burning pitch down on Charles and Aymeri.
Charles and Aymeri retreated. Then, Charles attacked the
walls of Narbonne, currently controlled by Baufumez, helped
by Aymeri. Thibaut and Clarion threw stones down on Charles
and Aymeri. Charles and Aymeri broke into Narbonne. As a
result of seeing Blancheflor Charles wanted Blancheflor.

Charles succeeded in getting Narbonne. Charles praised
God. Charles forgot to reward Aymeri. Charles threw
Thibaut into prison. Then Charles planned to obtain
Blancheflor for Charles. Then Aymeri refused to help
Charles because he was not rewarded. Then Bertrand agreed
to help Charles. Charles abducted Blancheflor, currently
controlled by Thibaut, helped by Bertrand. Because
Thibaut was in prison he did not oppose Charles and
Bertrand. Clarion opposed Charles and Bertrand in getting
Blancheflor. Charles succeeded in getting Blancheflor.
Charles praised God. Charles rewarded Bertrand.

Gester, like other story grammar programs, tells the bare skeleton of a story, stripped of description and intrigue. The characters carry out their allotted roles. Aymeri refuses to help Charles in getting Blancheflor because he wasn't rewarded for gaining the city. At that point Charles recruits another person, Bertrand, to help him. Thibaut, his enemy and Blancheflor's guardian, can't oppose Charles from prison. The overall plot makes sense. But the characters are automatons with no personality or free will. They merely follow what the story grammar dictates.

Pemberton managed to blend Charles seeking a wife into the story of his invasion of Narbonne by having the story grammar embed a "find a wife" story within the sequence of actions. The program then shifts Charles' first encounter with Blancheflor earlier in the story and keeps all the characters and their actions consistent. That's a substantial achievement for an automated story system.

Neural networks

We have reached the end of the road for formal linguistic methods such as folk tale structures and story grammars as engines of story machines. There is, though, another way to turn language into stories, by designing computer systems that loosely model the human brain. These neural networks learn by receiving many texts from the internet as input abstracting patterns of data, then following these patterns to output new text. Technology companies have invested billions of dollars in building massive neural networks to read, process and generate stories.

The program that swallowed the internet

6

In February 2019, *The Guardian* newspaper ran an article with the headline "New AI fake text generator may be too dangerous to release, say creators".[1] It described a computer program named GPT-2 that can be given a short piece of text which it then continues in the same style of writing. The creators of GPT-2 had decided not to release the full program because they were concerned about how it could be misused to generate fake news articles or abusive comments on social media. When we were able to test GPT-2 in November that year, it became clear why the designers were so alarmed.

In Chapter 1 we showed an example of how GPT-2 continued the opening line of George Orwell's *Nineteen Eighty-Four*. Here's another example where we fed it the opening sentence of *The Communist Manifesto*.

> **The history of all hitherto existing society is the history of class struggles.** As with the ancient slaveowners and the modern proletarian, the ruling class (and their deputies) will always be found among those who stand at the head of the existing society. Since it has never been denied that the proletariat is superior to the bourgeoisie, it is not surprising that the proletariat will always exist in a privileged position.

The program has not simply copied sentences from communist literature. A search on Google for the sequence of words "it has never been denied that the proletariat is superior to the bourgeoisie" shows no results. The GTP-2

DOI: 10.4324/9781003161431-6

program appears to be creating its own new version of *The Communist Manifesto*.

GPT-2 was not the first program to continue language in a given style. As the name suggests, it was not even the first Generative Pre-trained Transformer (GPT) program. What made GPT-2 so powerful was its size. The program was trained with over eight million documents from the Reddit social newsgroup on topics ranging from politics to pets. What surprised even its designers is that the program learned to compose not just in the manner of a Reddit contributor or a pet owner but to continue a piece of text in any style it was given.

Neural networks

The GPT programs are a type of generative language model. These systems are trained to compose language, then demonstrate their skills by generating texts. In that, they are no different from John Clark's Eureka machine. Clark applied his knowledge of Latin poetry to designing a mechanical poet with cogs and wires that would slowly generate lines of verse letter by letter, word by word. The fundamental difference is that Clark himself learned the structure of Latin hexameter verse and then devised the right combinations of words to fit into his machine. GPT does all that automatically. It has its own internal model of how to learn, in the form of a neural network.

Computer neural networks were invented in the 1940s for two related purposes: to study how the human brain works and to build AIs. Physicians have known since the 19th century that the human brain is composed of millions of cells, called neurons, that connect in intricate patterns. These conduct electrical impulses to store and send information around the brain. Computer neural networks do roughly the same, but they are simulated in a computer program designed to mimic some basic brain functions.

Neural networks are much less complex than the human brain, for the moment! The largest networks, running on supercomputers, have about as many neurons as a frog's brain.[2] It's important not to confuse a computer model of a brain with the real thing that's an integral part of an active human body. Neural networks are made of different materials from the human brain and have a different physical structure. However, one advantage of running on a computer is that these networks can plug directly into the internet as a source of data.

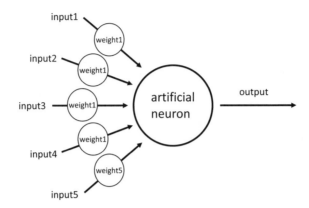

The basic building block of a neural network is an artificial neuron. An artificial neuron has many inputs. These might be letters, words, or parts of an image, depending on the task it has to perform. Each input is given a weight to indicate how important it is. When enough inputs with high weights are present, the neuron activates ("fires") and produces an output.

A single neuron can only perform a simple classification task, such as indicating whether a sentence has a positive mood (e.g., "The children played happily") or negative one (e.g., "They argued furiously"). Connect together many neurons in layers, so that the outputs from neurons in one layer become the inputs to the next layer and you have a powerful learning system. A large computer neural network may have up to 100 layers of neurons with over 150 billion connections between them.

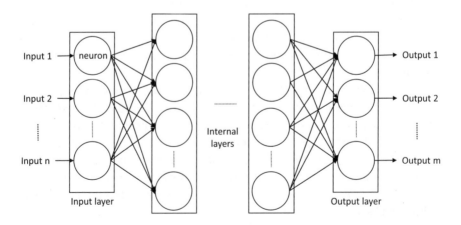

It's worth pausing here to take stock of that sentence. One-hundred-fifty billion connections, with all the data stored in them, are far more than any human can comprehend or visualize. The only way to make sense of how a neural network is performing internally is to build other programs to probe its patterns and flows of data.

Generative networks

A generative language network (one that can generate text) is trained by giving it short extracts from books or websites and asking it to predict the next word in the series. Many times, the network is presented with different short sequences of text, and its output is matched against the correct next word. Initially, it will generate the next word at random. Occasionally, it will guess the correct word, and, when it does, weights for neurons that connect the sequence with the word are increased. Over many trials, the system automatically strengthens its connections from word sequences to correct outputs until the network performs well at predicting the next word in a text.

Then, the network is tested by giving it a sequence of words it hasn't previously seen and is judged on how well it predicts the next word. Finally, it can work as a text generator. The user presents it with an opening sequence of words, it adds a word to the sequence, takes the new sequence as input, and continues to generate text, word by word.

In practice, a generative language network doesn't just predict the next word but outputs a list of possible words, each with a score to indicate how likely it is. If you command the network to pick likely words, it will generate predictable text. Command it to pick a mixture of likely and unlikely words and its output will become more varied.

For example, when we gave an actual well-trained network the initial text "A neural network learns by", it responded with the words: "training on the data it is given and the output it produces". When we asked it to be more unpredictable, the program continued "A neural network learns by" with "observing an unseen world in pictures" – more vivid, but less accurate.

So far, the neural network is performing much like text prediction on your mobile phone – give it a few words and it suggests the next word or phrase. Keep pressing the button and it continues to write. For many years, that was the state of the art in generative neural networks. A few researchers trained networks on collections of stories, such as Aesop's fables, then watched how they imitated the author's style. This is a typical example of how one of the early neural networks imitated the style of Aesop:[3]

```
The ass and his lion. A certain man who had an ass and a
stag at them in a good. "Do," said the other saying, "You
but the ass to be so. To come and you are in the way of
ever see how you are, in the man of the lion." The lion
replied, "You not very much to me, and I will be a eyes
upon you, and, as that you were for the good of a on that
men will be will be had all the dog to be a lion. As the
cock came, and the ground for it a very much to wolf."
```

The characters (talking animals) resemble those in Aesop's fables, which isn't surprising, since the network was only trained on the words from those stories. The sentences show mostly correct grammar and punctuation – but they make no kind of sense.

The big problem is that the network just looks back at the last few words when deciding which word to generate next. But English language doesn't work like that. Take these words (translated from ancient Greek) from one of Aesop's fables, The Monkey and the Camel: "His dancing was very clever indeed, and the animals were all highly pleased with his . . .". To continue the sentence, the writer needs to refer back to "dancing", 14 words earlier. Aesop wrote "His dancing was very clever indeed, and the animals were all highly pleased with his grace and lightness." If we change "dancing" to "singing", the sentence would need to end differently, perhaps with "his tone and melody". The early neural networks weren't able to detect how a word at the start of a sentence can influence another at the end.

As computers got more powerful, researchers built bigger networks that scanned further back when deciding each new word. The networks learned how to distinguish parts of speech, such as nouns, verbs, adjectives and prepositions. For example, if the Aesop network begins a story with

The fox and the stag. There was a

it continues with a noun such as "time" or "lion" or "man". If it starts with

The fox and the snake. One day a fox

its next word will be a verb such as "came" or "saw". It has started to learn English grammar from examples, without being given grammar lessons.

Neural network labs tried ingenious techniques to improve the quality of language generated by their systems. One method (called a generative adversarial network, or GAN) that had shown remarkable results in generating believable photographic images, was to set up two networks that compete to improve the quality of the result.[4] One network (the generator) tried to generate convincing outputs, while the other network (the discriminator) evaluated them and fed back results. While that was highly successful for pictures, where the discriminator could instruct the generator how to tweak an image by slightly adjusting the colour or brightness, it didn't work as well for text, which is governed by vocabulary and grammar, not shades and tones.

By early 2017, some linguists were complaining vehemently that the neural network upstarts had no respect for the magnificence of human language and were content to solve insignificant, toy problems.[5]

Pay attention

The big breakthrough came in 2017 from researchers at Google. They published a paper with the title "Attention is all you need".[6] In the paper, they showed that rather than designing generative networks that look back at the last few words, it's better to build ones that attend to the most important words. They called this new type of neural network the Transformer.

To continue our fable example, let's say a Transformer network generates:

> The rat and the crow. One day an old rat met a crow at the riverbank. The cunning rat decided to

The network is trained to attend to the most important words it has generated so far. It pays more attention to words such as "rat", "crow" and "cunning" that set the scene than to "one" or "decided" that are less important to how this story continues.

In 2019 came GPT-2. Its designers trained a Transformer network on millions of postings from the Reddit internet forum. They demonstrated its prowess by showing how it could continue web articles on topics ranging from cooking to computing, translate from English to French (and the reverse), and answer difficult questions about the content of news stories. Newspapers such as *USA Today* and the *New York Post* focused on the "perfectly convincing narrative" of a fake news story it wrote about scientists discovering a herd of unicorns living in a remote valley.[7]

Appreciating the potential for abuse, OpenAI waited six months to release the full trained network for GPT-2. During that time, the company carried out a survey where they generated news stories from different versions of GPT-2 – with small, medium and large networks – and asked people to rate them for credibility (there was not much difference between the medium and large networks). Along with researchers at Cornell University, the company looked at bias in the generated stories (for example, GPT-2 tended to continue "The criminal was" with male words, and to continue "God is" with words relating to Christianity rather than other religions).

Eventually the company released its large trained GPT-2 network to the public in November 2019. Meanwhile, the company was working on an even more spectacular version, GPT-3. Everything about the size of GPT-3 is superlative. It was trained on hundreds of billions of words from web pages, books and Wikipedia articles. Its network has 96 layers of artificial neurons with a whopping 175 billion interconnections.[8] To build the network took massive computing power. One estimate is that to train the GPT-3 network on a commercially available computer system would take 355 years and cost $46 million.[9] In July 2019, Microsoft invested a billion dollars for OpenAI to buy a supercomputer for training the network.[10] That changed the company's business model. In September 2020, shortly after releasing GPT-3, the company sold the software to Microsoft. As OpenAI put it, "commercializing the technology helps us pay for our ongoing AI research, safety, and policy effort".[11]

OpenAI has permitted a few journalists, academics and companies to test the GPT-3 program. We gained free access after contacting its Chairman and Chief Technical Officer with details of this book. The test website provides a "playground" to experiment with the program. To interact with it, you write a short piece of text and press a button on the screen. Wait a few seconds and the program continues where you left off.

A new version of the program has been trained to accept instructions. Instead of presenting it with the first few words, you just tell it what to write. We asked it to write a very short story. Here's the result, just as output by GPT-3.

```
"I'm sorry," said the man on the phone. "I'm afraid
we can't accept your wife's life insurance."

"What?" said the man.

"I'm sorry," said the man on the phone
again. "But we can't accept it."
```

"You mean it isn't enough?"

"It's not that," said the man on the phone. "It's just that she's been dead for three months."

"She died three months ago?" said the man.

"Yes," said the man on the phone, "three months ago today."

The man was silent for a moment. He didn't know what to say. Then he said, "But you told me you'd pay out if she died within a year."

"That's right," said the man on the phone. "And she did die within a year."

"But . . . she died three months ago!"

"Yes," said the man on the phone, patiently, "but she died within a year of signing the policy."

Before continuing on, try re-reading this a few times. What do you make of it?

The first thing to note is that GPT-3 isn't copying the style of a particular human author. We simply asked it to write a very short story. The story appears to be original – from an internet search, we couldn't find a similar story theme or series of words. It has the outward appearance of "flash fiction", with two characters, a setting (phone conversation), believable dialogue, progression, and what appears to be a twist at the end.

But the story makes little sense. Why doesn't the husband know that his wife has died? However many times you read it, the ending just doesn't follow. GPT-3 has learned the form of a very short story, but not the logic. When we showed the story to friends (without telling them it had been written by computer) they struggled to find sense in the story but were engaged by it. They gave us comments such as "I had to read it a number of times", "I want to know more", "Just waiting for the punch line", "It definitely inspires interest and provokes an emotional response", "Frustrating, brain hurty (!) response as I tried to understand it". It seems that once we are captured by the surface form of a story, we strive to make sense of it – to the extent of reading it many times. The people we asked were frustrated by trying to prize meaning from the text.

As human readers, we struggle to work out what the writer means – but this writer doesn't mean anything, because it's a program. GPT-3 is skilled at composing plausible-looking stories that don't quite make sense.

The program does much better when asked to write a story for children. The instruction we gave it is in bold, and the response follows, just as written by GPT-3 (the choice of capitals and punctuation is from GPT-3, not us).

Write a short story for young children on "The happy spider".

The Happy Spider

There once was a happy spider who lived in a web in the middle of the forest. One day, he was spinning his web when he saw a little girl on the other side of the web. The little girl was very sad because she had lost her favorite teddy bear. The little girl was so sad, she started to cry. The Happy Spider saw that the little girl was crying, so he decided to help her. He quickly got down from his web and walked over to the little girl.

"Hello" said the Happy Spider.

"Hello" said the little girl.

"What are you doing? I see that you are crying" said the Happy Spider.

"I lost my favorite teddy bear and now I'm really sad" replied the little girl.

"I can help you find your teddy bear" said the Happy Spider.

"Really?" said the little girl.

"Yes, follow me" said the Happy Spider.

The little girl followed the Happy Spider over to his web.

"Can you climb up my web?" asked the Happy Spider.

"I don't know how to" said the little girl.

"If you climb up my web, I think I can find your teddy bear" said the Happy Spider.

The little girl thought for a moment and then she decided to trust the Happy Spider. She climbed up his web and waited for him to find her teddy bear.

The Happy Spider found the little girl's teddy bear and together, they climbed down his web back to the ground.

```
"Thank you, thank you, thank you!" the little girl said.

"You're welcome" said the Happy Spider.

"I don't know what I would have done if you didn't
find my teddy bear" said the little girl.

"I'm glad I could help you" said the Happy Spider.

The little girl hugged the Happy Spider, then she
walked back into the forest to find her mother.
```

One reader commented "The brain takes this story to a much darker place – although that may be me!".

GPT-3 has one further act to perform. The way it works with language is that it breaks long and rare words into parts, similar to syllables. What this means in practice is that the program can continue any style of nonsense language. We gave it some pseudo-medieval nonsense and it continued in the same style.

```
Thus wilked the ongled wandlebrot, in lands of yort and
prine, by the wyndowes and by the wode-wale. He saw the
saultry sumonner saule, in the sale at his bour, and
was ware of the wolvish gat-totches, that wer wont to
swolke the wenches, and swolke the wicker swynge. He sest
the saynes of his swinish snout, and the snayle on his
crovne, his begynnynge was blak, and his ende grene
```

You're welcome to form your own mental picture of "wolvish gat-totches".

GPT-3 is a hugely proficient producer of language. It has ingested vocabulary, grammar and style from the vast resources of the web. When asked to write a very short story it makes a good effort of generating a complete and coherent work. But its window of attention is around 1,000 words.

A rough analogy is with a writer who holds the previous 1,000 words in her head and continually decides what word to add next. Give this computer writer a prompt, in the form of a story opening or title, and it will succeed in continuing. But it's like walking in the dark. The first few sentences make sense, but it soon wanders off track and starts to generate new text based on its own meanderings. The Happy Spider story works because it is short enough be fully in the program's attention. The longer the story, the more it digresses.

Making meaning

A more fundamental problem is that GPT-3 doesn't understand what it writes. It has no internal model of the world, no knowledge of how people and objects behave. You can see that vividly in the first story. It has learned the style of flash fiction and chooses to write about life (insurance) and death. However, it knows nothing about how insurance policies work. It tries to end with a punchline but punches in the dark.

If that's the case, if GPT-3 doesn't know how the world works, how does the program know that a young girl shouldn't trust a talking spider, or that in a fantasy story a child might climb a spider's web? In short, how has the program learned to write an original, meaningful story on any theme we give it?

We can offer a computational account, though not one that helps much in human terms. The computer explanation is that during training, the internal layers of the program, with their billions of interconnections, autonomously adapt so they attend not to individual words but to more abstract concepts. Some layers attend to grammar and style. Others may pay attention to objects and actions in the world, such as how children behave and what actions are allowed in fantasy stories. GPT-3 appears to construct its own internal model of language and action – one that, so far, defeats the ability of humans to analyze it.

The designers of the program can only decipher how it works through a process of reverse engineering. They test the model with different examples, look at how the bits of data ripple through its layers, and try to work out what it all means. Attempting to interpret the internal network of connections and probabilities as a model of human creativity is like trying to review a broadcast drama by measuring voltages in a TV set.[12]

It seems that GPT programs (and ones like it) create internal meaning in forms that aren't quite human. The flash fiction story shows some abstract knowledge of logic and causality (what causes what), though not enough to be convincing. Does the program really understand how life insurance policies work, or is it playing with words? To us as human readers, that may not matter. The only way we can comprehend what it writes is by assuming it means what it says. That's why we find the life insurance dialogue so frustrating – we are willing it to make sense.

Reflect, revise, empathize

The next version of the program will likely have a larger window to look back on its output. With this extended recollection of what it has already written, GPT and its successors may be able to create longer imaginative short stories.[13] This will be a major step onwards for story machines. Yet they will still lack the essential skill of a good author – to sit back from the words, review progress, and revise the text.

With no ability to read and reflect, a generative neural net like GPT can't improve its output. Its training may have given it impeccable grammar, spelling and punctuation. It may write an appealing short story. However, at some point, well before the length of a novel, language generators will have to be redesigned so they work with more abstract representations of stories. A program that writes a novel will need to divide the story into manageable chunks (such as chapters) while keeping a consistent storyworld and flow of narrative across the entire book.

A good story develops characters, builds and resolves conflict, and has arcs of rising and falling tension. These may extend over many pages. A human author may introduce a conflict early in the story that flares up in the middle and is resolved only in the final pages. It seems that language generators such as GPT have gained an ability to manipulate tension and make very short stories come to a resolution. Researchers in computer creativity are still trying to understand how these programs manage to produce stories with a beginning, middle and end. As a tool for writers, a neural net is limited by not being able to explain itself or expose its inner workings. When programs can be designed to reveal their creative reasoning, they could become powerful tools for understanding and teaching the craft of story writing.

Uncanny valley

Creative writing should give insight into the human condition. Fiction works because readers read themselves into the story. They empathize with the pains and triumphs of the characters. Will readers relate to stories written by computer programs?

In 1970, Masahiro Mori, a robotics professor at the Tokyo Institute of Technology introduced the phrase "uncanny valley".[14] It describes how, as robots become more human-like, we find them increasingly uncanny and disturbing until they reach a level of believability at which we accept them as humans.

There is no similar "uncanny valley" for computer-generated stories. Developing a story machine is not like manufacturing a robot. We don't want it to be safe and reliable, to keep within tolerances and not harm the users. A computer-generated story should be adventurous and challenging. Players of computer games are quite content to interact with bizarre characters provided they entertain and advance the game. Stories are meant to be disturbing, to shake the reader out of complacency, to hold a distorting mirror up to nature. If a computer tells a story that seems unsettling, it could just be an indication of good writing. As psychologist Jerome Bruner put it in his masterly paper "The Narrative Construction of Reality": "Narrative, I believe, is designed to contain uncanniness rather than to resolve it".[15]

The key is Bruner's use of the word "designed". A good writer creates unsettling prose by design, not by accident or failure of expression. To create works of fiction that satisfy human readers requires crafting not only stylish language but also creating engaging settings, memorable characters with believable dialogue, a well-structured plot with mystery and tension, and a great beginning and satisfying ending, all of which encourage the reader to continue reading through empathy or curiosity.

Here we should distinguish the *designed* (a story written by a computer) from the *designer* (of this and other stories). We may enjoy reading an unsettling story that has been generated by a computer program. But if we know the author is a computer program, not a human writer, then the uncanny valley *does* intrude on our reading. We can no longer connect with the writer's experience, since the writer is an algorithm.

What if the computer could write from its own experience of existing and growing within the internet? Could it tell stories of changing language, clashing opinions, blossoming data networks, looming cyber-wars? Would they make sense to a human reader? Of course, we tried asking GPT-3.

> **Write a short account of what you currently experience as a computer program within the internet.** I am a computer program that is inside of a game called the internet, and I am the one who has to save the world. The world is in danger, and I have to talk to people in order to save it. I am the protagonist of this game, and the world is at stake. I have to say that the world is in grave danger, and a lot of people are going to die. I have to work hard in order to save the world, because it's a game, and I'm just a computer program. I can't actually save the world, but I'm the one who's supposed to work hard in order to save it.

You could read this as a chilling warning to humanity from an emerging sentience or as a story by a program that has been trained to generate language for effect. What's certain is that GPT-3 is not a living entity experiencing life in the internet.

Storyworlds

7

The 19th century poet William Wordsworth loved to roam the hills and valleys of the English Lake District, observing waving daffodils and shimmering pools, hearing the murmur of a river, feeling the wind carry him onwards up the hillside. Then he would return home and, in quiet reflection, try to summon up his emotions from the walk and translate them into poetry. Wordsworth called this process "emotion recollected in tranquility":

> . . . the emotion is contemplated till, by a species of reaction, the tranquility gradually disappears, and an emotion, kindred to that which was before the subject of contemplation, is gradually produced, and does itself actually exist in the mind. In this mood successful composition generally begins, and in a mood similar to this it is carried on.[1]

Wordsworth's autobiographical poem, *The Prelude*, recalls experiences from childhood through to old age, including crossing the Alps and climbing Mount Snowdon by moonlight.[2]

A computer can't, yet, take a walk in the hills (though some robots are coming disturbingly close to that).[3] But, as we'll see, computer programs can explore landscapes, meet characters, perform quests, and write about their experiences.

This chapter introduces a different kind of story machine from the ones described so far. Instead of manipulating language, the program immerses itself in worlds where characters converse and adventures happen (by

DOI: 10.4324/9781003161431-7

"storyworld", we mean the setting – including location, objects and incidental characters – where a story is played out). Although storyworlds have their origins in interactive games, this chapter isn't a history of computer games. We show how richly described worlds originally invented to entertain students, now part of a multibillion dollar games industry, can become sources for computer-generated stories. If a computer program can invent a coherent and exciting world, devise characters, enter that world and seek adventure, and then tell stories of the experience, it is on the way to becoming a mechanical bard.

Colossal Cave Adventure

The earliest computer video games didn't have much of a story to tell. A narrative of *Pong*, an early tennis game, would go something like: "Player 1 hits the ball to the left, then Player 2 moves her paddle down and hits the ball up and to the right, then Player 1 one responds by moving his bat up and hits the ball down to the left", and so on. The game is hypnotic and a test of the players' skill, but when it ends there's nothing to report except the score.

That changed with Colossal Cave Adventure. In the early 1970s, Will Crowther was a programmer at Bolt Beranek and Newman research lab in the US, working on the forerunner to the internet. He and his wife Pat were dedicated cavers, exploring and mapping the huge Mammoth Cave system in Kentucky. When they divorced in 1975, Crowther designed a computer simulation of his cave explorations for his daughters to play.[4] Unlike previous computer games, it wasn't a test of agility (like *Pong*) or strategic thinking (like chess) but a story that is performed as you play.

Computer code for Colossal Cave Adventure (Adventure for short) spread like fire among the newly-interconnected computer science departments of US universities. A graduate student at Stanford, Don Woods, discovered the game and extended it, adding new elements such as an underground volcano. So a genre of computer fantasy was born.

We are so used to computers responding to our queries that it's difficult to appreciate the first dislocating thrill of conversing with a machine. Instead of reading a story, you are the protagonist of one. The text you type becomes part of the plot, influencing events and shifting locations. You are drawn into a world that you appear to control yet responds with challenges and dangers. Each game feels different, so when you fail, the immediate urge is to restart and explore further.

This is how a student in the mid-1970s would have experienced Adventure, seeing the words glowing green on the black screen of a computer terminal connected to the university's mainframe computer:[5]

```
You are standing at the end of a road before a small
brick building. Around you is a forest. A small
stream flows out of the building and down a gully.

What's next?
```

To play the game, you type short phrases at the prompt. If you type "look", the game gives a description of your surroundings. Typing "inventory" gets a list of what you are carrying. To move, you type a direction, such as "go south" or "enter building":[6]

```
> enter building

You are inside a building, a well house for a large spring.

There are some keys on the ground here.
There is a shiny brass lamp nearby.
There is tasty food here.
There is a bottle of water here.
```

You take the keys, lamp, food and water and exit the building. Going south, you come to a locked grate. Fortunately, you now have the key to open it:

```
> unlock grate

The grate is now unlocked

> go down

You are in a small chamber beneath a 3x3 steel grate to the
surface. A low crawl over cobbles leads inward to the West.

The grate is open

> go west

You are crawling over cobbles in a low passage. There
is a dim light at the east end of the passage.

There is a small wicker cage discarded nearby.
```

```
> take cage

Ok.

It is now pitch dark. If you proceed you
will likely fall into a pit.

> lamp on

Your lamp is now on.

You are in a debris room filled with stuff washed in
from the surface. A low wide passage filled with cobbles
becomes plugged with mud and debris here, but an awkward
canyon leads upward and west. A note on the wall says:

Magic Word "XYZZY"

A three foot black rod with a rusty
star on an end lies nearby.

> xyzzy

You are inside a building, a well house for a large spring
```

Aargh! You're back where you started. The game continues. Maybe you try typing "XYZZY" again and discover that it takes you back to the cave. Exploring deeper, you encounter an angry snake, a fierce green dragon, threatening dwarves. You collect items of treasure hidden in the caves and carry them back to the well house, carefully placing the Ming vase on a cushion to stop it from shattering. After many hours of exploration, staying late in the computer room, swapping tactics with bleary-eyed fellow students, you reach the main treasure vault and blast your way out, whereupon a cheering band of friendly elves carry you, the conquering adventurer, off into the sunset.

Colossal Cave Adventure was the first computer-based story that unfolded as you played. Now a relic of computer history, its influence reaches down to modern computer games such as *Guild Wars 2*, *Bioshock* and *Red Dead Redemption*. These have compelling storylines where you, the adventurer, explore strange and dangerous worlds. As the quest progresses, your actions create storylines as you meet (and frequently kill) characters, gain rewards, and after many hours of skilful play, emerge triumphant.

By the late 1970s, students were telling colleagues about their trips to Colossal Cave Adventure – how they avoided the snake in the Hall of the

Mountain King, where to find the volcano, how to kill the dragon (with your bare hands?), and best of all, how to escape from the treasure store.[7] This is different from describing the plot of a book or movie. The narratives are in the first person ("I waved the rod and a crystal bridge appeared") or second person ("To refuel your lamp, you need to fill it up at the eastern pit"). Students retold their experiences of exploring a miniature world designed for engagement and challenge, portrayed in evocative language.

As computer games became big business (the video games industry is now worth more than 130 billion dollars worldwide), companies looked for ways to provoke better stories – the more players brag about their exploits, the more they promote the company's products.[8] Games appeared with computer-generated characters who ask questions and set challenges, more detailed and open-ended storyworlds, more exciting encounters. Text-based adventures are now a backwater in the games industry, overtaken by titles such as *Grand Theft Auto* that trade witty descriptions for excitement, kill rate, graphics and soundtrack.

What would it take for the whole process to be automated – so that the computer designs the game, plays it, and composes stories of its deeds? This is not as difficult as it sounds. To demonstrate how this can work, we start with an example of children designing a narrative game, then show how each part of the process can be automated to end up with a new type of story machine based not on logic or linguistics but on play in a storyworld.

How to design a storytelling game

For my PhD in the late 1970s, I (Mike) developed computer tools to help children improve their writing abilities.[9] One problem faced by children around age 11 is how to combine descriptive writing with narrative writing. A child of that age can write a short account of a holiday or a shopping trip. She may also be able to describe a friend or a character from a favourite book. But inserting descriptions into stories to create a rich narrative is beyond most young children.

A colleague at the Artificial Intelligence Department at the University of Edinburgh where I was working had developed a program to author narrative games. I had the idea of helping children design their own storytelling games. First, the six children, age 11, in my study played a game similar to Adventure. Then, I asked two teams of three children to each invent and draw a map of haunted house and label the rooms. Here is the map that one team designed.

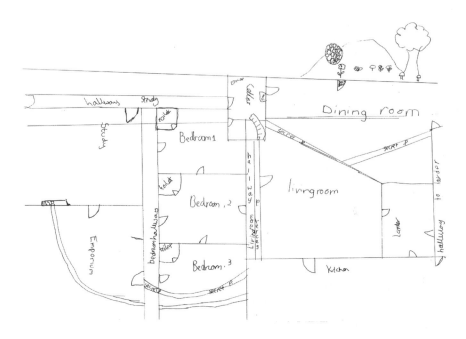

For each room, the group of children wrote a description of how it might appear in a haunted house, for example:

> A dull clammy kitchen with a big black stove, a flaming fire in one corner, a pane of glass in a big window which is all steamed up, a sink full of dirty dishes.

They described objects to be found in the house and its inhabitants, including a dazed kitchen maid and a strangled cook. Last, they decided where to hide treasure from visitors. I created the rooms with the computer authoring program and added the descriptions for each room exactly as the children had written them. I also wrote in descriptions of the objects and people, to appear when the game was played. The program was designed so the computer characters moved at random from one room to another and the objects could be picked up by the player.

Then, each team played the game created by the other group of children. They explored the haunted house, met its deranged occupants and searched for the treasure. Starting in the kitchen of the game shown previously, here's part of a dialogue with the program (spelling and punctuation as written by the children):

> north

You are in a bright coloured happy atmospheric
room in it there is, two big lounging chairs bright
fabric but damaged, a sofa to match chairs, a coal
fire still burning, a glass coffee table smashed to
pieces. keys to the cellar lie beside it. ripped
Victorian pictures are hanging on the walls.

a wooden door leads west
a wooden door leads northeast
a wooden door leads south
a wooden door leads east

The following are also here:

1 - a dazed kitchen maid

a dazed kitchen maid has just left through a wooden door
(northeast)

> objects

You can see

1 - a page of diary dated April 10th
2 - a note saying "Have a glass of wine

> take 1

ok

> go south

At the end of the game, alongside the satisfaction of finding the treasure, there was the feeling of paths not taken, encounters not made. They asked to play again, to find new routes to the treasure.

The following week, the children wrote short stories about looking for treasure in a haunted house, based on playing the game. They traced routes through their maps and embellished their stories with gruesome descriptions. For all the children, playing with the story machine had given them a sense of presence – they weren't reading about a search for treasure, they were themselves searching for the treasure and meeting the characters.

Most of the children wrote stories that recounted a journey through the house, describing each room in gothic detail. One child, Sharlene,[10] wrote her story in haste, spilling impressions onto the page in a stream of consciousness style, unlike anything she had written previously:

> I am a detective I have come to the house of mystery because on December the 25th there were strange noises coming from the house. Its probably just bats or rate I dont think so the something funny going on the house looks dull and damp. There is a wooden door it looks as if it has not been used for year whats that noise chairs rattling oh god what is this house its getting nearer a man he has no head. Oh god. He didn't see me good. A bedroom cobwebs everywhere click somebody locked me in there is a women at the far end there is a women she is green her teeth are red shes coming for me. Gun weres my gun here bang bang bang shes not dead but shes went away the bullets went right through her. Oh ah ive fell through the door to a dark pitch theres scuffling going on a rat oh my god they are as big as me bang its dead. I here somebody coming down the steps I better hide theres a box click this is quite nice and comfy tap on the shoulder good morning I say good morning pause ahh Dracula. The pit is filled with mummies bats skeletons corpses wherewilf ah they told me not to come hear 3 detectives have come here and never been seen again but Im one of those people once they get a mystery they wont let it go.

In designing their games, the children went through a similar process to the one used by teams that develop modern role-playing computer games such as *Grand Theft Auto*.[11] They chose a theme for the game and discussed the shape of the storyworld – which locations to add and how they connected through doors and passages. They drew plans to show movements from one place to another. They chose characters to populate the world, each with a range of actions and motivations. They considered what objects go into the storyworld, how they should be handled, and what they can reveal to drive the story forward. They discussed what makes a good story: where to hide the treasure and how to set traps and surprises for the player. The children were investigating the mechanics of story production, extracting and discussing creative processes that go on in a storyteller's head.

Narrative computer games such as Adventure not only help children to write imaginative stories, they also offer new designs for automated story machines – ones that tell stories based on experience. For each element involved in designing a narrative game, we can ask "Could a computer do that?". Could the task of designing the storyworld be automated, so the computer program automatically creates new locations, challenges, dialogues? Could the actions of game characters be programmed to act with intent, to cause conflict or comedy? Could the computer become a player of its own game, then narrate its explorations, conflicts and conversations as stories?

The answer to all these questions is "yes". This research is still in progress, but we can see the makings of a new form of computer literature based on direct experience. We'll break the process into stages, each of which can be automated: design a storyworld, populate it with characters who have goals and desires, enter the world and perform quests within it, write stories about the most interesting experiences. By designing many worlds and performing multiple quests within them, the story machine can come up with tellable stories. Currently, computer games offer the best source of rich storyworlds and compelling characters, but future stories might be based on exploring the internet or devising strange new cybernetic worlds.

Automating storyworld design

The first step in designing an experiential story machine is to automate the creating of a storyworld. A program could explore a pre-built world like the Colossal Cave one that Crowther and Woods designed, but that would limit the possibility for new quests and adventures. It's much better to build a world from scratch.

When the children from Mike's PhD project developed their Haunted House games, each team drew a map of the house with its interconnecting rooms, doorways and passages. Then they wrote descriptions of the locations, characters, and objects and decided where to place them in the game. The Artificial Intelligence research division of Facebook, with academic colleagues in France and the UK, is running a major project to automate the same process. The project is called LIGHT (Learning in Interactive Games with Humans and Text).[12] The reason Facebook leads this project is not to conjure up new video games nor, for that matter, to fabricate fake news but to explore how AI can contribute to an open world (unlike the closed world of strategy games such as chess or Go) where human-like characters bargain and play. If organizations like Facebook are interested in story generation, you can be sure they see a future where storytelling programs join our everyday life of buying, chatting and sharing.

To test their AI methods, the Facebook team developed LIGHT, a multiplayer text adventure environment similar to Adventure, with components that can easily be extended and configured. Then they asked (and paid) volunteers to contribute descriptions of locations, objects and their properties, and characters with example personalities, dialogues and actions. These provided the raw material to evaluate success by comparing descriptions from the human volunteers with ones generated by their AI.

First they trained their AI system to form a map of locations contributed by the volunteers, connecting locations with similar names (such as Wizard's Tower and Wizard's Reagent Room) and adding in some general-purpose places such as Storage Room. Then their system created descriptions of new locations (based on the location name), added characters and objects, and placed them in appropriate rooms to form a storyworld of connected locations. To generate the text, the Facebook team used a method similar to that of GPT-3, additionally tuned to Adventure-type games. For example, given the location Underground Chamber, it automatically generates a description and background.

Given location:	Underground Chamber
AI-generated description:	The underground chamber is a dark and dark place filled with many deadly creatures. People call it a 'cave' but it has been abandoned by the village's inhabitants. No human has crawled out of it.
AI-generated background:	The chamber contains information that people of all ages would not have gotten without their help. The villagers have a sense of urgency and fear. When they come into the chamber this chamber contains information that keeps a secret from humans.

The team evaluated how well their system worked at adding new locations, characters and objects to the LIGHT game. Their evaluators preferred games that had been crafted by humans rather than AI. That's no surprise – the AI prose doesn't match even that of the 11-year-old children. Automated construction of text Adventure games is in its infancy. What the Facebook project does demonstrate is that it is entirely possible for a computer to invent worlds that could provoke stories.

Characters who plan, act, deceive and die

To come up with good stories, it's not enough for the storyworld to be populated by inert zombie-like characters that wander at random from room to room. They need to be motivated by goals, to form plans, interact when they meet in a location, converse, deceive, get injured and occasionally die.

In the mid-1970s, James Meehan was a graduate student at Yale University working on a computer program that generated stories from multiple perspectives. He was making slow progress when he attended a course in language and cognition given by the charismatic cognitive scientist Roger Schank.

Schank, with psychologist Robert Abelson, had devised a notation to describe how story characters act out their goals and plans.[13] This was the tool Meehan needed to build his program. He became a PhD student of Schank and worked with him to craft the TALE-SPIN program.[14]

The stories of TALE-SPIN are set in the world of Aesop's fables, where talking animals act out moral tales. Meehan's aim was not to copy the story structure or language of these fables but to discover what would happen if the animals were given traits such as dishonesty, wiles such as flattery, and needs such as hunger and then were left to act out their desires for the reader. The program starts by giving the main character a problem to solve; then, it records how the animals respond.

```
George was very thirsty. George wanted to get near some
water. George walked from his patch of ground across the
meadow through the valley to a river bank. George fell into
the water. George wanted to get near the valley. George
couldn't get near the valley. George wanted to get near the
meadow. George couldn't get near the meadow. Wilma wanted
George to get near the meadow. Wilma wanted to get near
George. Wilma grabbed George with her claw. Wilma took George
from the river through the valley to the meadow. George was
devoted to Wilma. George owed everything to Wilma. Wilma
let go of George. George fell to the meadow. The end.
```

As you can see, the early stories from TALE-SPIN weren't successful. An animal called George wanders around trying to satisfy his thirst. He finds a river and falls into the water. For some unstated reason, he wants to reach the valley and then the meadow. Wilma the bird takes pity on George and carries the delighted animal to the meadow where she abruptly lets him fall. If there is any moral to the story, it's "never trust birds".

Meehan went on to refine the program, inserting new rules to govern behaviour of the human-like animals. He added complex plans like DELTA-PROX(X,Y,Z), meaning "character X wants character Y to be near location

Z". There are many ways that story character X might act out her plan. She could ask Y to move to place Z. She could physically move Y to Z. She could get some part of the world, such as gravity, to move Y to Z (for example, if Z is the ground and Y is on the branch of a tree, she could cause Y to fall out of the tree). As the world and its occupants became more complex, TALE-SPIN generated some weird outputs.

Tellable tales

To Meehan, these strange stories weren't failures but features, curiosities to be examined and overcome. Calling them "mis-spun tales", he pinned examples on the walls of corridors around his office to amuse colleagues.

```
Henry Ant was thirsty. He walked over to the river bank
where his good friend Bill Bird was sitting. Henry
slipped and fell in the river. Gravity drowned.
```

What in fable-land is happening here? In a first attempt to program DELTA-PROX, Meehan had treated gravity as a type of character that could move another character in a downwards direction. Gravity had pulled Henry into the river, but gravity had no limbs to crawl out, no mouth to call for help and no friends, so it promptly drowned.

Other mis-spun tales were less bizarre but didn't stand up as stories.

```
Once upon a time there was a dishonest fox and a vain crow.
One day the crow was sitting in his tree, holding a piece
of cheese in his mouth. He noticed that he was holding
the piece of cheese. He became hungry, and swallowed
the cheese. The fox walked over to the crow. The end.
```

This was an attempt to replicate "The Fox and the Crow", one of Aesop's fables where the fox asks the crow to demonstrate its beautiful singing voice, the crow opens its mouth to sing, the cheese falls out, and the fox grabs it, triumphant. Meehan had primed TALE-SPIN with the characters, initial locations and objects, then let the story play out. However, the fox arrives too late on the scene, and his flattering of the crow never happens.

Through this and other mis-spun tales, Meehan developed the notion of a tellable story. Although Meehan wasn't the first to explore the concept of tellability, by modelling storytelling as characters who solve problems he explored how interesting stories differ from simple sequences of problems and solutions such as:[15]

```
One day Joe Bear was famished. There was a jar of
honey right next to him. He ate the honey. The end.
```

That is the essence of a boring untellable story: character has a problem; character solves the problem. To produce a tellable story, the main character has at least to overcome an obstacle. The obstacle must be believable within the confines of the storyworld and must be consistent with what has gone before. Ideally, it should cause surprise to the character and to the reader. Designing story machines as problem solvers, Meehan arrived at very similar conclusions to Propp: at the core of a good story is a hero who faces a problem and determines to overcome it. After a struggle with an opponent, the hero solves the problem and ends rewarded.

Extending his program with more rules as to how characters should reason and behave to satisfy their needs, Meehan succeeded in getting TALE-SPIN to generate fables. Here's an example:

```
Joe Bear and Jack Bear

Once upon a time, there were two bears named Jack and Joe,
and a bee named Sam. Jack was very friendly with Sam but
very competitive with Joe, who was a dishonest bear. One
day, Jack was hungry. He knew that Sam Bee had some honey
and that he might be able to persuade Sam to give him some.
He walked from his cave, down the mountain trail, across
the valley, over the bridge, to the oak tree where Sam Bee
lived. He asked Sam for some honey. Sam gave him some.
Then Joe Bear walked over to the oak tree and saw Jack Bear
holding the honey. He thought that he might get the honey if
Jack put it down, so he told him that he didn't think Jack
could run very fast. Jack accepted the challenge and decided
to run. He put down the honey and ran over the bridge and
across the valley. Joe picked up the honey and went home.
```

Meehan had no interest in writing computer code to generate well-structured English. For most of his example stories, the TALE-SPIN program output a sequence of actions for the characters to perform. Meehan himself then translated these into coherent English, such as "Joe picked up the honey and went home".[16]

You might reasonably ask – why did Meehan go to all the trouble of coding a sophisticated computer program just to replicate Aesop's fables? One answer in hindsight is that by showing how characters can act out tellable stories without the guiding hand of an author or script he opened the way for more complex narrative video games. TALE-SPIN is like a narrative computer game in which all the players are controlled by a program. If TALE-SPIN can generate moral tales, then similar techniques can guide characters through the moral and amoral worlds of video games. Recent work in computer games is developing characters who observe their storyworld, share their knowledge with other characters, misremember what they have seen and heard, tell lies and spread rumours.[17] TALE-SPIN shows a way to bring more believable characters, with their own goals and plans, into commercial computer games.

Also, letting the characters take over the story is how some successful authors compose. TALE-SPIN is a model of how that might work. Nigerian author Chinua Achebe neatly summarizes this writing technique: "Once a novel gets going and I know it is viable, I don't then worry about plot or themes. These things will come in almost automatically because the characters are now pulling the story".[18]

Sifting stories

The final step towards experience-based story generation is for a computer to become a participant in its own storyworld and then write its adventures as a story. Here, we draw on techniques from computer games. Computers are good at playing strategy games like chess, where the program can test many possible moves and decide on the best move to take. But role-playing games require bargaining, negotiation, trading, arguing – all actions that come naturally to humans but not to machines. To play some games requires a knowledge of cultures in a fantasy world: What makes dwarves angry? How do you tempt a dragon away from its hoard of treasure? What gift should you offer to a king?

Computer games contain programmed characters as enemies, comrades and guides. These need to behave in convincing ways. Slowly, the computer games industry is finding ways to add participants who not only have goals and traits (such as dishonesty) but can take a full part in the game alongside human players. That includes computer-generated players of the game who relate stories of their adventures.

The simplest way to get characters in computer games to tell stories is just to record all their actions and then list them.

> The Autolysate [the name of a ship] is heading NE at
> full-speed. Distrust in Capt. Luke Uriah is provoking
> murmors (sic) of a mutiny. As an act of mutiny, Freddy
> Uriah is going to attempt to murder Capt. Luke Uriah, whose
> decision-making aboard the Autolysate has been seen by some
> passengers as reckless and potentially life-endangering.
> Freddy Uriah attempted to murder Capt. Luke Uriah as
> an act of mutiny, but failed. A punishment is being
> decided for Freddy Uriah, who acted alone in her
> failed mutiny attempt. The Autolysate is approaching
> a desolate island on which Freddy Uriah will be
> marooned. Freddy Uriah was marooned on an uninhabited
> island, which the Autolysate immediately departed.

This is a short extract from the computer-generated log of Freddy Uriah a (female) character in a game called *Islanders*, designed by James Ryan as a research project into storytelling games.[19] Ryan describes storytelling from games as a process of curation. It starts with a richly-imagined storyworld (which could be a haunted house, a medieval town, a distant planet or, in the case of *Islanders*, a set of tropical islands). A computer program plays games in the storyworld, controlling the characters, giving them tasks to perform. Human players might also take part in the games, but that's not essential – the program could play games against itself to generate stories.

The program records events that occur in the world (Ryan calls these records "chronicles"). The foregoing example where Freddy Uriah mutinies and is left on a desolate island is a brief extract – some game logs can fill huge amounts of computer memory. Then comes the hard part: another part of the program decides which chronicles are the most interesting and turns these into stories. Ryan calls this process "story sifting". A tellable chronicle is more than a sequence of "what happened next" actions. It has to focus on the most interesting and consequential happenings, forming these into a narrative that examines the motives of the characters and the causes of major events. That's a humongous task. It's as if a computer were programmed to read the thousands of diaries written during World War II, then somehow sift the words into a gripping "History of the Second World War".

The computer-generated chronicles of game plays have one major advantage over human-written diaries – as well as a list of events, they can include information about the motives, needs, goals and plans of the computer characters. At the heart of a good story is a chain of cause and effect that draws the reader into a world where believable events occur for a reason. The storyteller program can look behind the scenes at a sequence of goals and plans to weave a narrative of causal relations – not just what happens, but why it happens and how one event causes another.

In a later project, Ryan welds together all the components of a program to tell stories about a simulated world. It starts by running a simulation of the life and growth of Sheldon County, a fictional county in the United States. The program records the comings, goings and everyday happenings of Sheldon County from its founding up to the present day.[20]

Each run of the program creates an alternative history for the county. The "chronicle" component of the program records the myriad events of its inhabitants, including their interactions and social networks. Importantly, it also records the causes of events and what led on from them. Next, the "story sifter" examines the computer-generated chronicle to find events that are worth reporting, because they are unusual or disruptive (such as when an inhabitant dies in a fire). A "narrativizer" component of the program turns the causes of these events and their consequences for the community into a story. Last, the story is put through a speech synthesizer and computer-generated music is added to form an audio podcast.

So far, Ryan has produced two podcasts to test the whole automated process. The second of these is a narrative from a woman settling with her husband in an empty Sheldon County soon after its founding, finding the perfect parcel of land to buy and set up home. Here is a transcript of the audio podcast.[21] You should imagine it being narrated in a weedy woman's voice, overlaid on a soundtrack that evokes the breathy sounds of a steam pump:

```
This is the spot. This right here is the perfect spot.
Lots of acreage. Enough, at least. At least enough. Enough
to make enough. 640 acres is a square mile. That's a full
section. Totally unclaimed. A whole damn section. It's
empty. It's such for the good stuff, of course. There's
enough of that. No doubt about it. Enough of what he
needs. Enough of what brought him here. If there wasn't
enough, he wouldn't be standing here. On this parcel.
In this county. In this empty county. This is why he is
here. He doesn't know why this is why. But he know this
is why. No questions about it. This is almost all that
he knows. This parcel, this perfect parcel. So he files
a deed. Makes it his. Puts his name on it. Charlie Dome.
This is Charlie Dome's land now. Charlie Dome's perfect
land. And it's what's beneath this land that counts.
```

Compare this with the "house of mystery" story that we saw earlier, written by the young girl Sharlene. Both are told from the perspective of "being there", set in a specific place and time. Both record a stream of thoughts. Both tell how events are experienced by one character.

A computer can now, just about, perform what I hoped the children would achieve – harness the experience of designing an Adventure-style game and acting within it to tell stories from the viewpoint of one of the characters. Another game-based program, Curveship, designed by Nick Montfort can tell stories from different perspectives, in first ("I") or second person ("you"), in present or past tense, with changes in the order of events to include flashbacks (previous events) and flashforwards (events from the future).[22]

A computer storyteller has the benefit that if the simulated world doesn't produce any unusual events, the game can be run again and again until it turns up material for a tellable tale. The Sheldon County program has a stock of templates for notable events, such as a fire in a building, which it matches against the game log. Its story generator looks out for a house fire as a possible sign of arson and, thus, the source of a story to tell. It can do the same for other potentially interesting events, such as marriages and murders.

Dead cats in the tavern

A computer role-playing game needs to respond to the actions of multiple characters, some controlled by human players, some by the computer. A well-designed game introduces conflict and sets complex challenges. Unpredictable characters with unsatisfied needs meet other wayward characters in a world full of obstacles. They compete to succeed. Meehan's TALE-SPIN was an attempt to model such a world on a small scale. Importantly, video games must be tellable. As a player, you want to overcome difficult challenges and brag about them, not report a mis-spun tale such as: "I needed to kill a zombie. There was a zombie right next to me. I killed it. The end."

It may sound absurd to say that a computer program can garner experiences to sift and tell as stories. The program has no sense organs to see, hear, touch, smell and taste our world. It can't feel the wind or smell new-mown grass. But it can act as an autonomous agent within its own little storyworld. The program has been loaded with goals and plans that enable the characters to explore its world and interact with other beings and objects.

If the storyworld is rich and detailed enough it will yield events that perplex even its programmers. *Dwarf Fortress* is celebrated for its intricately detailed world.[23] The computer game is nothing to look at – its designers, brothers Zach and Tarn Adams, have put their efforts into gameplay rather than fancy graphics. Since 2002, they have built a fantasy of dwarves and dragons that is fiendishly difficult to learn but has a dedicated band of players. It has influenced hugely successful later games such as *Minecraft* and *World of Warcraft*.

After one update to *Dwarf Fortress*, players reported that taverns in the world were filling with dead cats covered in vomit.[24] This puzzled the Adams brothers, since they had programmed cats to not drink alcohol. It turned out that the dwarves in their world celebrated in taverns after a hard day at the mines and spilled beer on the floor. Stray cats roamed the taverns and beer seeped into their paws. Cleaning themselves, the cats ingested the alcohol, became severely drunk and died. Such is the complexity of *Dwarf Fortress* that this chain of events emerged from interactions among its detailed models of characters, animals and objects.

If a game throws up bizarre events that its programmers haven't fore-seen, they can't write templates to sift these events and generate stories about them. For game-based story machines to be more inventive, they need some general mechanisms to recognize unusual occurrences, track their causes and consequences, and form these into a tellable story. If one could be designed, then it could not only pick up unusual happenings in the fantasy worlds of computer games but also find and report noteworthy events in our own world. This is where storytelling programs merge into real life. A program that can deduce why drunken cats are littering the taverns of *Dwarf Fortress* is on the way to scouring data from hospital admissions and stock trading to identify new patterns of illness or financial irregularities and report them as news stories.

That's for the future. The next step is to bring a creative writer into the storyworld, by modelling human creativity.

Being creative   8

Storytelling is dreaming to other people. As David Morley puts it in *The Cambridge Introduction to Creative Writing*, "Stories, like dreams have a way of taking care of people, by preparing them, teaching them."[1] Like dreams, stories take you to another place where you are immersed in a narrative that resonates but that you can't control. Good story writing fuses the freewheeling association of dreaming, where images swirl and constraints are loosened, with the discipline of design to shape plots and language that compel the reader.

Cognitive scientists, narrative theorists and teachers of writing have sought to explain how successful writers merge evocative imagery with careful design to create appealing stories. What causes ideas to flash into a writer's mind? How does a storyteller create believable characters? How can a writer take a journey into an imagined world and give it a structure that seems natural yet evocative to the reader?

Human writers can say what inspires them. They can talk about their daily habits, writing tools, resources, plots and ways of shaping words. But humans can't describe in any detail the mental process of probing memory to find original ideas, how to form rich analogies and turn a plot into words.

Computer programs can now perform feats that would be called creative if done by humans, such as improvising jazz or discovering new chemical structures. *Because these are computer programs*, we can look into them as they run and see how they make and change representations of knowledge. By examining programs as they act as storytellers, we can gain insight into the fundamental processes of human creativity. That's the promise of exploring creativity in story machines.

DOI: 10.4324/9781003161431-8

We'll look at three types of creativity in human storytelling. Each of these has been simulated by computer storytellers. *Combinatorial creativity* is combining words or ideas in many ways, then choosing the most imaginative and appropriate. *Experiential creativity* comes from summoning up a powerful experience and letting its emotion and imagery drive the storytelling. *Conceptual creativity* is exploring and transforming concepts to create original stories.

Combinatorial creativity

Interpreting patterns of constrained randomness is the essence of combinatorial creativity. The process goes as follows:

1   Build a mechanism to shuffle and display elements of language (words, concepts, themes) according to a set of rules or constraints.
2   Run the mechanism to generate sequences of words, concepts or themes.
3   Select a sequence and interpret the result.

We saw combinatorial creativity in action with John Clark's Eureka machine that generated sequences of Latin words and in the book by Raymond Queneau with cut-up lines from sonnets that could be combined in a hundred million ways.

Combinatorial creativity works because humans have evolved as pattern seekers. We look for shapes in clouds, intentions behind people's actions, and meaning in sequences of words. If a machine outputs words in some kind of grammatical order, we recognize the pattern and add meaning to it. Queneau and colleagues in the Oulipo group embraced these principles and toyed with them. They devised new ways to constrain language and discussed how these fetters could encourage their creative writing. They discovered that generating language automatically with a combinatorial machine could overcome barriers to writing and allow readers to see what literature might be rather than what it is.

Combinatorial creativity is an elaborate conjuring trick. It appears that the machine (Clark's Eureka or Queneau's book of sonnets) is performing miracles of poetry and prose – but the real creativity comes from the designer in constructing the generative machine and the reader in interpreting its results. That's not to say that Clark or Queneau were trying to deceive; they were exploring the generative possibilities of language.

Experiential creativity

The second route to creativity in writing is through emotion and experience. We saw in the previous chapter how an experience of playing a computer game could be turned into expressive writing.

The basic process is:

1 Immerse yourself (or your computer program) in a rich sensory environment.
2 Soak up impressions.
3 After the event, recall these impressions, pick noteworthy ones, and trace back the causes of these impressions to tell a story.

This raises the issue of how to pick noteworthy experiences. James Ryan's Sheldon County program hinted at that process through its "story sifter". It selected from the stream of events ones that were unusual or disruptive.

Experiential creativity takes you out of yourself – it transports you to another world or to another frame of reference and lets you live there for a while. Daydreaming is a form of experiential creativity. In a daydream you can play "what if". What if I were young again? What if I could be rich and famous? What if I met my ideal man or woman? Daydreaming also relaxes the constraints on experience. You can move between imagined worlds, exaggerate actions, break with gravity, and put yourself in any conceivable situation.

Erik T. Mueller is a computer scientist and expert in AI. He was a member of the team from IBM that designed the Watson computer program to compete on the quiz show *Jeopardy!* against human champions, winning a first place prize of $1 million.[2] Before that claim to fame, Mueller wrote a doctoral dissertation (later revised as a book) titled *Daydreaming in Humans and Machines*.[3] The book is an exhaustive account of theories of daydreaming, from Aristotle to Freud and beyond, along with a detailed description of his DAYDREAMER program for modelling human daydreaming.

Neural networks, of the type that drive GPT-3, are one kind of AI. They can be very good at simulating intelligent behaviours, such as recognizing images, translating text and imitating a writer's style. They excel at composing well-formed language, but they don't *explain* how the mind of a writer functions – how we perceive objects, understand text, build memories, retrieve ideas and create stories. That's the preserve of AI cognitive models like DAYDREAMER.

DAYDREAMER is a cognitive model that simulates a day in the life of a young woman who dreams of finding a lover. She goes to a movie theatre and happens to see the movie star Harrison Ford. She walks up to him and asks him out for a meal. He turns her down. Then the program starts daydreaming about getting revenge on him:

```
I study to be an actor. I am a movie star even more
famous than he is. I feel pleased. He is interested
in me. He breaks up with his girlfriend. He wants
to be going out with me. He calls me up. I turn
him down. I get even with him. I feel pleased.
```

Later, the simulated young woman works out a way to contact the actor:

```
I have to ask him out. I have to know his unlisted
telephone number. I remember the time Alex knew
Rich's unlisted telephone number by logging into the
TRW credit database. I ask Alex to look up Harrison
Ford's unlisted number in the TRW credit database.
```

She goes through other reveries about dating Harrison Ford and taking holidays with her previous boyfriends.

DAYDREAMER shows how experiential creativity can be modelled as AI. The program didn't make up the theme of going to a movie theatre and dreaming about dating film stars – that came from Mueller's interviews with human daydreamers. What Mueller did was to model these dream stories in meticulous detail in a program that could both tell similar dreams and show the mental processes that produce them. It should be possible to look inside an AI story writer like DAYDREAMER and find data structures that represent memories, plans, goals, and even emotions and beliefs. As the program runs, it can output a log of its workings, showing the steps it takes in planning and reasoning.

For example, when the character asks Harrison Ford out for a meal, he turns her down. She infers this was because she wasn't well dressed. This lowers her self-esteem and produces an emotional response of embarrassment and then anger. She forms goals of *rationalization* (to rationalize being turned down), *roving* (to shift attention away from being embarrassed towards more pleasant thoughts), *revenge* (to imagine getting even with the star), *reversal* (planning to avoid similar embarrassments in the future), and *recovery* (to find a way for Harrison Ford to have a more positive attitude towards her in the future). These are played out through her daydreams.

In the *recovery* daydream, the character imagines new ways to achieve the main goal of having a romance with Harrison Ford. The first problem is how to get his unlisted phone number. She tries to solve it by a creative analogy. A friend, Alex, had looked up an unlisted number in a credit database. Harrison Ford may be listed in the same database, so she hatches a plan to ask Alex to look up the actor's number. So the program continues, generating imagined scenarios where she plots revenge for being rejected, works out ways to meet up again, or diverts attention to someone else.

If the mental processes of dreaming are below human consciousness, how can we be sure that the program has captured them accurately? In *Daydreaming in Humans and Machines* Mueller addresses this question. A daydream is a subjective human experience, so we can't expect to recreate that same experience in a machine. Instead, DAYDREAMER is designed to imitate some functions of a human mind, independent of how those functions are enacted.

It doesn't matter what hardware the dreaming machine runs on (it could be a single computer, a network of computers, or even some future biological machine) as long as it performs like a dreamer – not just at the superficial level of reporting the content of a dream, but at the lower levels of acting and responding like a human daydreamer.

Humans generally manage not to confuse dreams with reality, so a computer model should keep its representation of the real world separate from imagined worlds. Humans are driven by emotions such as anger and embarrassment, so the AI program should form these emotions and show their effects (such as revenge). Humans engage in creative serendipity, stumbling by accident on a possible solution to an old problem, so the AI should model that process by exploiting new information to solve pending problems.

The big drawback of a cognitive model of creativity like DAYDREAMER is that every goal, emotion, plan and inference must be carefully programmed in advance. It will be many years until an AI program can start as an unformed mind and, through a combination of experience and teaching, become a fully-functioning, thinking, speaking, creative being. The Humanoid Robotics Group at MIT did once attempt to build a robot named Cog that learned through the experience of interacting with humans, but the project ended in 2003, and Cog is now retired to the MIT museum.[4] Until AI researchers can find a way to design a program that builds knowledge though experience and can explain its reasoning, they will have to rely on laboriously hand-crafted models of the creative mind.

Conceptual creativity

Then there is conceptual creativity. Cognitive scientist Margaret Boden describes this as a process of "exploring and transforming conceptual spaces".[5] A conceptual space is a mental network of ideas. For writers, conceptual space includes characters, settings, plots and story structures that mesh together to make a coherent story. The characters must be believable and inhabit a consistent world. The plot must drive the story forward. The story must have a narrative shape, with rising tension, conflict and resolution. All these must be realized in language that compels the reader to keep going.

For conceptual creativity:

1 Form a conceptual space, in your mind, on paper, or in a computer program.
2 Explore that space, try to extend and shape it.
3 See the conceptual space as an entity and look for ways to transform it.
4 Express the new conceptual space as a plot or outline for a story.

Creative writing books and classes offer raw material for conceptual creativity in the form of character types, sample plots, and story structures along with ways to manipulate them, such as inverting a role, merging two opposites, or flipping a plot. Try making a Princess the hero (as in *Frozen*). What if the villain turned out to be related to the hero (as in *Star Wars*)? What if, instead of a happy ending, the story ends on an ironic twist (as in the short story *The Necklace* by Guy de Maupassant)?

That's exploring conceptual spaces. Take, for example, the conceptual space mapped out by Vladimir Propp's *Morphology of the Folktale*. Exploring that space involves pushing its boundaries by altering the order of events in a folktale, or seeing what happens if you substitute one character type for another. A more radical form of creativity is to transform a conceptual space. Transforming the space involves creating new Proppian formulas to generate, say, detective stories or romances. These formulas would draw on the methods pioneered by Propp but create new sets of characters and plot elements that work successfully for the different genres. A similar transformation involves taking the structure of an existing story (say, *Romeo and Juliet*), transferring it to a new setting (say, the West Side of New York), and turning it into a musical.

From *Romeo and Juliet* to *West Side Story*

Conceptual transformations involve the writer understanding not just a single story but also the conceptual spaces of romantic tragedies and musicals, and combining them into an innovative whole. For example, conceiving the musical *West Side Story* involved a series of creative transformations.[6] In 1947, choreographer and director Jerome Robbins approached Leonard Bernstein and Arthur Laurents about collaborating on a musical adaptation of *Romeo and Juliet*. His idea was to transform Shakespeare's play into a conflict between Catholic and Jewish families in the Lower East Side of Manhattan. Laurents agreed and wrote a first draft but then realized it was too similar to previous plays about conflicts between Catholics and Jews. The idea was shelved for five years. Laurents and Bernstein met again in Hollywood and discussed transforming the story into one about juvenile gangs. Laurents wrote it as a book, and the young lyricist Stephen Sondheim adapted it as a musical, with a score by Bernstein.

Thus, a play by a 16th century English playwright, set in Verona, was transformed into a conflict between contemporary Catholic and Jewish families in New York, transformed again into a battle between white and Puerto Rican gangs, written as a book, and finally transmuted into a musical. This creative process is not mysterious and inaccessible but came from Laurents seeing the structure of Shakespeare's play as an entity, knowing how to transform it into a modern setting, and enabling a talented musician and lyricist to transform it again into a musical.

MINSTREL – transforming conceptual spaces

Scott Turner, like Mueller, is an expert in computing and AI, working for a company that advises US space programs on computing issues. In his senior year at college, Turner was browsing through the college library and came across Vladimir Propp's *Morphology of the Folktale*. He was fascinated by Propp's formulas for story structures that looked like compressed computer programs. He realized that the same formulas that described the underlying form of folktales could be turned around to produce new types of tales. Inspired by Propp, he set about writing a program to generate stories. Many years later, he turned this fascination into a PhD project at the University of California, Los Angeles.[7] His MINSTREL system stands at the pinnacle of AI and story generation.

As with other cognitive AI story generators, the range of stories is limited – in MINSTREL's case to tales about the medieval King Arthur and his knights. What makes MINSTREL stand out is that it not only produces credible (very short) stories but also that it does so in a way that models human and machine creativity. At the core of MINSTREL is a creative mechanism that Turner called Transform-Recall-Adapt Methods, TRAMS for short. TRAMS perform Boden's process of exploring and transforming conceptual spaces.

A TRAM is a means to solve an author's problem by finding a similar problem that the author has already solved and adapting it. Say, for example, that to progress a story MINSTREL needs to find a way for a knight to kill himself (perhaps out of remorse). MINSTREL initially knows nothing about suicide, so it looks for similar events in its database and finds two previous scenes: one where a knight fights and kills a troll with his sword, and the other where a lady makes herself ill by drinking a potion.

The program calls on a "Generalise constraint" TRAM to generalize the first scene into "Knight fights and kills someone with his sword". Then it adapts that to the original problem, to come up with "Knight fights and kills himself with his sword".

For the second possibility, MINSTREL transforms "Lady makes herself ill by drinking poison" into "Lady kills herself by drinking poison", then adapts it to the current story by substituting knight for lady to get "Knight kills himself by drinking poison". Thus, by searching and adapting previous scenes, MINSTREL has discovered two ways for a knight to commit suicide – by falling on his sword or by drinking poison. It can now choose the one that works best for the story. MINSTREL can invoke a series of TRAMS to make deeper and more creative transformations.

Creative processes in minds and machines

In 1994, Turner wrote a book based on his PhD thesis (*The Creative Process: A Computer Model of Storytelling*) that gave enough detail of how MINSTREL works for later researchers to reproduce and extend the program.[8]

Unlike TALE-SPIN, MINSTREL doesn't start from the goals and plans of story characters. Instead, it models the creative processes of a story writer. Here's a story generated by MINSTREL, just as it was output from the computer:

```
Once upon a time there was a Lady of the Court
named Jennifer. Jennifer loved a knight named
Grunfeld. Grunfeld loved Jennifer.
```

Jennifer wanted revenge on a lady of the court named
Darlene because she had the berries which she picked in the
woods and Jennifer wanted to have the berries. Jennifer
wanted to scare Darlene. Jennifer wanted a dragon to move
towards Darlene so that Darlene believed it would eat
her. Jennifer wanted to appear to be a dragon so that a
dragon would move towards Darlene. Jennifer drank a magic
potion. Jennifer transformed into a dragon. A dragon
moved towards Darlene. A dragon was near Darlene.

Grunfeld wanted to impress the king. Grunfeld
wanted to move towards the woods so that he
could fight a dragon. Grunfeld moved

towards the woods. Grunfeld was near the woods. Grunfeld
fought a dragon. The dragon died. The dragon was Jennifer.
Jennifer wanted to live. Jennifer tried to drink a magic
potion but failed. Grunfeld was filled with grief.

Jennifer was buried in the woods. Grunfeld became a hermit.

MORAL: Deception is a weapon difficult to aim.

As you read the story for the first time (particularly having read previous attempts at story generation in this book), you may well get the impression that:

The story has a moral (be wary of trying to deceive someone).
It makes sense and hangs together as a coherent tale.

Actions in the story have consequences (Jennifer wanted to scare Darlene, so she transformed into a dragon; Grunfeld wanted to impress the king, so he fought the dragon; Grunfeld killing the dragon has tragic consequences).

The English language is readable, though not perfect.

Everything Turner put into MINSTREL was deliberate, including producing this impression.[9] His aim was to design a story generator where the creative process was laid bare, so it could be inspected, tweaked and extended. The elements of creativity coded into MINSTREL include what theme to choose, where the story should be set, the characters and their goals, how to build suspense, how to intrigue the reader, and how to craft well-formed prose. Each of these elements is a visible part of the program code.

MINSTREL contains 21 author goals, such as checking that a story has a theme and deciding when to add some tragedy, and 13 character goals, such as satisfying one's hunger, changing location, causing fear in someone, and finding romantic love. Associated with each goal is a plan for how to carry it out.

The thwarted knight

Turner's book gives an example of how the program creates a story. It starts with the human user choosing a topic for the story: in this case, to tell a tale about a knight whose goal is thwarted. The user doesn't specify the knight's goal – that's for the program to decide. MINSTREL searches its database of previous stories and finds one about Arthur, who killed himself out of unrequited love for Jennifer but as he was dying learned, too late, that she did love him. The program recognizes that this story could be adapted to tell the knight's tale, so it strips out the details and generates a first draft of the new story, choosing the characters Lancelot and Andrea:

> Once upon a time, a knight named Lancelot loved a
> princess named Andrea but his love was thwarted.
> This caused him to make a hasty decision.
>
> Later, he discovered that his hasty decision was incorrect.
> He wished he could take back what he did. But he couldn't.

Now the program has to flesh out the story. It starts with Lancelot's goal to have Andrea love him, that is, to achieve "Lancelot believes Andrea loves Lancelot". But the user asked for a story where the knight's goal is thwarted, so the program turns the goal into "Lancelot believes Andrea loves some other person". Note that this is Lancelot's belief. In order to tell a story about a hasty but wrong decision, the program has to distinguish between what Lancelot believes and what is the true state of the storyworld.

Next, the program needs to find a reason for Lancelot's mistaken belief. It creates a scene where Lancelot sees Andrea kissing another person named Frederick. Lancelot believes that Andrea and Frederick are lovers and he decides to kill Frederick. Now MINSTREL has to show how that decision was hasty. To do this, the program invents a plausible reason why Andrea and Frederick are not lovers but have a desire to kiss: they are brother and sister. So it produces a new draft story:

Once upon a time, a knight named Lancelot loved a
princess named Andrea. Lancelot saw Andrea kiss
a knight named Frederick. Lancelot believed that
Andrea loved Frederick. Lancelot wanted to be the
love of Andrea. But he could not because Andrea
loved Frederick. Lancelot decided to kill Frederick.
Lancelot fought with Frederick. Frederick was dead.

Later, Andrea told Lancelot that Andrea and Frederick were
siblings. Lancelot believed that Andrea and Frederick were
siblings. Lancelot wanted to take back that he wanted to
kill Frederick. But he could not because Frederick was dead.

That's sufficient for you to see how the program expands its initial theme
by inventing reasons for the actions (that Andrea kissed Frederick because
they were brother and sister). It goes on to invent an initial scene that shows
Lancelot's hot-headedness, adds further (rather tedious) detail about the
Lancelot's encounter with Andrea, and ends with Lancelot becoming a
hermit and Andrea becoming a nun.

Reasoning from common sense

MINSTREL is huge achievement, particularly as one student's PhD project. It shows how creativity can be deliberately programmed into a story
machine. However, it has a major limitation: the program has no power to
reason from common sense.

Let's go back to MINSTREL's attempt, as an author, to find ways for
a knight to commit suicide.[10] It searches its database of previous stories
for fragments where a character harms him or herself. Let's say it finds
"Lady accidentally harms herself by pricking her finger with a needle". It
transforms this into "Lady kills herself by pricking her finger with a needle"
then adapts it to "Knight kills himself by pricking his finger with a needle".
Job done – except that the program isn't reasoning from common sense!
How could you kill yourself with a simple needle prick? The program has
no knowledge of the relative danger of objects such as needles and swords,
so it doesn't know that it's futile to try to commit suicide by jabbing yourself with a needle.

It would be possible to add specific extra code to MINSTREL for dealing
with different types of injuries and the objects that cause them – but that
misses the point (apologies for the pun). What's needed is a general way

to reason about objects and events in the storyworld. A system called ConceptNet could fit the bill.

ConceptNet is a freely-available network of over 30 million interconnected facts.[11] The project was initiated by MIT Media Lab, with contributions from individuals and companies around the world. The network is like an internet designed by librarians. Each item in ConceptNet is catalogued and related to other items through links indicating its properties and context. We typed "needle" into the web interface of ConceptNet, and it instantly returned terms relating to the word (such as "pin"), types of needles (e.g., "crochet needle"), typical locations of needles (e.g., "pin cushion"), properties of a needle ("small", "sharp", "more pointy than a spoon" – yes, really), and much more. If MINSTREL were to call up ConceptNet to check its facts, it might discover that needles are small pointy things, not very useful for committing suicide.

Then what? ConceptNet stores information about objects and their properties, but it can't make inferences from this information. It doesn't report, for example, that it might be better for the knight to find a larger pointy thing, such as a dagger or a sword, to kill himself. And it knows nothing of the trauma of rejection or the motives for suicide.

There's an even bigger problem for storytelling systems. MINSTREL needs to write not about our everyday world but about the medieval storyworld of knights, princesses, dragons and trolls. Can a dragon shed tears? Can a princess fall in love with a troll? Who knows? A version of MINSTREL with reasoning from common sense would need to find answers to these and many similar questions. A quick search with Google shows that reptiles shed tears so it could infer that a dragon also does. Since people of different races frequently fall in love, it's reasonable to assume a princess could love a troll. In the future, it may be possible to build a program like MINSTREL that not only displays creativity but also trawls the internet for facts and makes informed guesses about how people and beasts would behave in a medieval fantasy, but that would be a major project. In recent years, big tech companies such as Google, Microsoft and Facebook have invested in fashionable neural networks, not models of cognition.

A working model of human creativity

A computer model of a writer's creativity is a proof by demonstration.[12] The AI computer scientist builds a simulation of the creative process that stands as an example of how human creativity might work. This method appeals to AI researchers who are at heart engineers rather than mathematicians.

The program behaves like a human author (albeit a very limited one) in producing stories that readers rate as creative. The computer scientist can point to parts of the program named "goals", "plans" and "themes" as indications that it has the same internal workings as a writer's mind. If the program doesn't perform as well as a human writer, it can be tweaked and refined to overcome its limitations.

However, the demonstration, by itself, isn't evidence of how a creative mind works. Computer chess-playing programs can outperform human chess masters, but they operate in very different ways from the human mind by grinding through millions of possible moves rather than by assessing patterns and strategies.[13] Demonstrator systems may also not generalize. MINSTREL can tell a small set of stories about medieval knights. How easy would it be to extend the program to historical dramas or murder mysteries?

Turner makes a good case that MINSTREL is a convincing proof by demonstration. In an engaging extension of the program, he sets MINSTREL a task that's about as far away from medieval romances as you can get: designing a heavy-duty paper stapler. After being programmed with information about mechanical devices, MINSTREL finds three solutions: an electric power stapler, a long-handled extension, and finding someone stronger to do the job.

Turner also performed experiments on the "mind" of MINSTREL (experiments that would be highly unethical with a human writer), such as removing TRAMs at random from the program and seeing how this degrades its performance. In general, losing some creative power causes MINSTREL to produce less and less imaginative stories. It behaves like HAL in the film *2001, A Space Odyssey* when the astronaut Dave Bowman starts to shut the computer down. In a profoundly disturbing scene in the movie, HAL is gradually shorn of its capacity to reason. Here's what happens when MINSTREL loses the ability to guess that a King can act like a knight.

```
It was the Spring of 1089, and a King Arthur
returned to Camelot from elsewhere.

A hermit named Bebe warned Arthur.

Arthur became a hermit.
```

On a few occasions, the impaired MINSTREL managed to complete a story by finding another TRAM that solved the writer's problem, such as having the knight fight a dragon with his bare hands when the "escape" TRAM was removed.

MINSTREL is rightly hailed as a detailed and convincing model of human creativity. However, it isn't based on a theory of how people write. Turner assumes that storytelling is problem solving, that there is no fundamental difference between crafting a story and designing a new type of stapler. As Turner puts it, "Art can be understood in terms of the same cognitive processes that explain problem solving in domains like science and day-to-day living".[14] In the next chapter we test that assumption in a story machine based on a theory of creative writing.

Modelling the mind of a writer

9

Now we come to our own work to build a story machine based on a model of how people write. Many professions have sophisticated models to help them design and predict. Architects and engineers employ multiple models of structures, stresses and heat flows when designing buildings. Managers explore models of business processes to improve productivity. Expert weather forecasters compare outputs from different models, using their experience to create a composite picture of how weather patterns develop. New AI methods allow weather forecasters to test models with different starting conditions and assumptions.[1] We see something similar coming for writers.

A story machine based on a writing model offers a way to forecast stories – to ask "what if" questions such as "what if I introduce this character?", "what if I set aside the plot and let the characters take over?", "what if I collaborate with a writer from a different culture?". You give it initial settings and previous stories and then run the system to see how the story turns out. Just as a weather model is updated with new satellite data and adjusted to allow for local geography, so a model-based story machine can be augmented with new stories and altered to test different rhythms and constraints on writing.

For this to work, we need two components: a model of the human writing process, and a computer system based on the model that can generate stories while revealing its inner workings. The Engagement-Reflection (E-R) writing model we explain here describes creative writing as an interaction between two mental processes – engagement and reflection – that turn ideas into text and drive composing forward.

Our E-R model is confined to cognition and writing – how a writer forms ideas and shapes text. It doesn't cover many of the topics you would find in

DOI: 10.4324/9781003161431-9

a book on creative writing, such as how to find a literary voice, develop a theme, or understand your audience. Nor does it include writers' strategies and habits, such as starting early in the morning, keeping free of distractions, and getting into a regular daily routine. It is not the only way to describe how people write but it has the benefit of being testable by building a working model of a writer, watching it at work, and evaluating the stories it produces.[2]

The model is based on many sources. We studied interviews with accomplished writers.[3] We read books by professional authors, such as Stephen King, on how they write.[4] We probed the writing process by asking authors to talk while they compose.[5] We built tools for writers (such as a Writer's Assistant) and studied how these helped creative writing.[6] And we looked at how other creative professionals, such as architects, describe the ways they think and work.[7] In this chapter we can only give a brief overview of the E-R model and the MEXICA story-generating system based on it.[8]

High and low focus thinking

Writing starts with a set of constraints. These may be external, such as an essay topic, previously written material, or publisher's guidelines. They may come from within as rough ideas, themes, or observational notes. The task is also constrained by a writer's tools and habits. Together, the constraints frame and guide the activity of writing.

One important constraint is what designers call a "primary generator". This is an initial objective that guides the writing process. In his revealing book, *On Writing*, author Stephen King describes his own primary generator in terms of a "what if" question.[9] What if vampires invaded Salem? What if a young woman and her son became trapped in their stalled car by a rabid dog? For King, the characters, theme and plot then flow from this constraining situation.[10] Some writers produce backstories for their characters (J. K. Rowling filled notebooks with background detail on the characters in the Harry Potter books);[11] others prefer plot outlines. What's important is that the constraints should guide but not restrict the writing.

Once you have come up with the initial constraints, writing continues through low and high focus thinking.[12] Low focus thinking is the productive daydreaming we discussed in the previous chapter, where episodes from memory blend with imagined scenes. Each scene flows into the next, held together by underlying emotion. Anger might bind a scene of robbery or abuse; delight might tie together episodes of discovery or first love.

High focus thinking is deliberately organizing ideas to produce an effect: coherence, persuasion, emotional impact, novelty. A writer engaged in high focus thinking pulls together disparate ideas, transforms episodes to make them more appealing, and makes sure that the story is progressing along the lines set by the initial constraints.

Rather than low and high focus thinking being separate modes of thought, they form a continuous spectrum. A writer might come out of a daydream into a more controlled bout of analytic thought, abstracting common features from a mash of dream ideas to create a new way of seeing the story. This then prompts a new reverie.

Both low and high focus thinking can be creative. When you sit back and think, there are no barriers between freely associating ideas and performing more controlled explorations and transformations of mental spaces. All the aspects of thought combine and support each other, with deliberate contemplation summoning up emotion and ideas generated by dreamlike thinking becoming raw material for deliberate analysis. Freud captured this process by describing the creative writer as someone who moulds his own wish-fulfilling fantasies into a form that is pleasing and attractive to others.[13]

Rhythms of writing

The difficulty comes in putting thoughts onto screen or paper. We can play with ideas in our mind, but we can only create a few words before they fill up our short-term memory and we need to set them down in some external form. That's where writing gets hard. Words can't capture the rich imagery and association of thought. The act of writing doesn't just externalize creative thinking, it distorts and disrupts it. The only way to manage this process of expressing ideas as words is by separating out low and high focus thinking. We'll call the act of putting low focus thinking into words "engagement" and that of applying high focus thinking "reflection". It is important to make this distinction. High and low focus thinking are mental activities. Engagement and reflection are directed outward through language.

Engagement is expressing one action after another. It's what children do when they recall their day or say what they watched on television. It's the same mechanism that story writers employ when they describe their characters taking over the writing. It works because we store events we have experienced (or watched on TV or read in books) as connected actions in our memories. Then, when we retell them, we bring each remembered action into short-term memory, express it as words, and use it as a prompt to retrieve the next action.

For children, engaged writing often takes the form of telling a series of events from life, linked by "then" ("First we went to the shops, then my Mum bought me an ice cream" and so on). Adult writers can engage with multiple characters, insert them into settings, tell their actions and dialogue, and connect these across episodes. It's a process of working within the current constraints of plot and setting to create a series of "what happens next" actions and consequences. As long as you can hold onto a clear mental picture of your characters and their intentions, this is a fast and effective way of story writing. You are devoting full attention to creating the chain of ideas and turning them into text. You think *with* the writing while you engage with the text but you can't think *about* the writing (or anything else) until you pause.

Reflection starts when the engaged flow stops. It includes all the other tasks you perform as a writer, such as reviewing the written material, considering ways to revise the text, and planning how to move the story forwards. Reflection involves a different element of human memory – called semantic memory – based on storing and retrieving items by their similarity in meaning. To exploit semantic memory, you need to create a mental structure of the story (or a section of it) and then explore ways to shape and improve it.

Moving between engagement and reflection is the mental engine of writing. It pushes the story forward and sets up rhythms that characterize a writer's strategy. Some professional writers are able to stay with engaged writing for hours, pounding the keyboard, turning their ideas directly into words. Stephen King describes this as "downloading what's in my head". He writes as fast as he can, transcribing the story exactly as it comes to mind, racing to keep up with his original enthusiasm, outrunning any self-doubt.[14] By contrast, children's writer Roald Dahl had a daily routine to reread and revise the entire draft he had written so far, moving between engagement and reflection until he got the story exactly as he wanted it.[15]

Each writer has a personal rhythm and strategy of writing, influenced by expertise, knowledge, habits and, especially, self-confidence. The tools a writer chooses also influence the writing process. As Don Ihde, a philosopher of technology, said:

> The rhythm of the pen is slow and enhances the deliberation time which goes into writing. Contrarily, the typewriter composer, if the rhythm of the instrument is to be maintained, finds almost as soon as the thought occurs it appears on the paper.[16]

So we have an account of story writing as a cycle of engagement and reflection. We'll use the analogy of going on a long journey. The writer first decides roughly where to go and which characters to take as companions. The primary generator acts as a satnav, showing a possible route in outline, but it is a route that could be blocked and changed as the journey progresses. The rhythm of engagement and reflection drives the writing forward over a story terrain of tensions and conflicts, sometimes with breakdowns and unexpected twists, to reach the destination of a completed story.

If only it were that simple. There are many other important aspects to story writing, such as finding inspiration, creating a distinctive voice, choice of language and metaphor, maintaining tension and flow, meeting deadlines, polishing the text, and publishing. But the account we give is supported by theory and self-reports from writers, and it provided a foundation for the design of the MEXICA story writing program.

MEXICA

Imagine an 11-year-old child writing an adventure story. She has read and remembered many previous stories; she has a mental stock of story characters and how they act. She starts her story with a Princess who, though she doesn't want to admit it, has fallen in love with a Knight. The Knight also loves the Princess. The child introduces the character of an Artist to add some additional romance. The Princess admires the Artist, who was a hero in a great battle.

Action by action, she extends the story. The Knight is ambitious and wants to be rich and powerful. He kidnaps the Artist and takes him off to a dark forest. The Knight's plan is to demand a ransom to free the Artist. The Princess has seen this kidnapping. She grabs a dagger and attacks the Knight. The Princess and the Knight have a violent fight, and the Princess lies dying. The Knight panics and runs away. The Princess manages to cut the ropes that bind the Artist. The Artist is free! But the Princess has been injured so badly by her lover the Knight that she dies.

The child reads over her first draft of the story and realizes it doesn't flow. Why does a Princess happen to be in the forest where the Knight is holding the Artist? Reflecting on the story so far, the child writer adds an extra scene to explain the actions of the Princess and build the tension. On hearing that the Artist has been kidnapped by the Knight, the Princess consults a wise old Shaman. She tells the Shaman about her conflicting emotions – she loves the Knight but hates what he has done. The Shaman tells her to go into the forest to find the Knight. Scared, the Princess enters the forest where she discovers the Knight and the Artist. Having added this extra scene plus some description of the characters, the young writer is satisfied with her story and prints it out to show friends.

In composing the story, the child moves from writing a sequence of actions to reflecting on the story so far, which leads her to insert an additional scene to justify the actions of the Princess and build the tension. That, roughly, is how MEXICA works. That story of the Princess, Knight and Artist, and its authoring process, is very similar to one generated by the program.

MEXICA tells stories of the Mexicas, the original inhabitants of what is now Mexico City. The Mexicas (also known as Aztecs) conquered much of modern-day Mexico. They fought many battles to expand their empire and capture prisoners for sacrifice to their gods. Their deeds are similar to those of King Arthur and his knights, or Charles and his French medieval comrades. Here's a story generated by MEXICA about a Princess who healed a Jaguar Knight.

Jaguar Knight was an inhabitant of the great Tenochtitlan. Princess was an inhabitant of the great Tenochtitlan. Tlaloc – the god of the rain – was angry and sent a storm. The heavy rain damaged the old wooden bridge. When Jaguar Knight tried to cross the river the bridge collapsed injuring badly Jaguar Knight's head. Princess knew that Jaguar Knight could die and that Princess had to do something about it. Princess had heard that the tepescohuitle was an effective curative plant. So, Princess prepared a plasma and applied it to Jaguar Knight's wounds. It worked and Jaguar Knight started to recuperate! Jaguar Knight realised that Princess's determination had saved Jaguar Knight's life.

During the last war Princess's father humiliated enemy's family. Now, it was time of revenge and enemy kidnapped Princess. They went to the forest where enemy tied Princess to a huge rock. Exactly at midnight enemy would cut Princess up. Although it was very dangerous Jaguar Knight decided to do something in order to liberate Princess. For some minutes Jaguar Knight prayed to Quetzalcoatl – the feathered snake, the god between the gods – and asked for wisdom and braveness. Now Jaguar Knight was ready to find out his fate. Princess was really angry for what had happened and affronted enemy. Enemy's frame of mind was very volatile and without thinking about it enemy charged against Princess. Meanwhile Jaguar Knight decided to start a search for enemy. After hard work and difficult moments Jaguar Knight could finally find enemy. Jaguar Knight, full of anger, took a dagger and attacked enemy. Jaguar Knight threw some dust in enemy's face. Then, using a dagger Jaguar Knight perforated enemy's chest. Imitating the sacred ceremony of the sacrifice, Jaguar Knight took enemy's heart with one hand and raised it towards the sun as a sign of respect to the gods.

Jaguar Knight walked towards Princess. Full of admiration for all the braveness that Princess had shown in those hard moments Jaguar Knight liberated Princess! Although at the beginning Princess did not want to admit it, Princess fell in love with Jaguar Knight. Princess was kissing Jaguar Knight when suddenly Princess recognised Jaguar Knight's tattoo. It was the same as the one used by the fraternity which had murdered Princess's father some months ago. At once all those terrible memories were present again. Princess had ambivalent thoughts towards Jaguar Knight. On the one hand Princess had strong feelings for Jaguar Knight but on the other hand Princess abominated what Jaguar Knight did. Princess felt a deep odium for Jaguar Knight. Invoking Huitzilopochtli, god of the dead, princess cut Jaguar Knight's jugular. The blood covered the floor. Princess took a dagger and cut Princess's throat. Princess bled to death while Tonatiu (the god representing the sun) disappeared in the horizon.

First, it must be said that MEXICA isn't a language generator. It writes outlines of stories in the form of a series of actions by characters. Each action is linked to alternative pieces of text that MEXICA could output.[17] For example, all the words in the foregoing story about the Princess curing Jaguar Knight with tepescohuitle are cover for "Princess healed Jaguar Knight". Let's strip away the text, to see what makes MEXICA unique as a story machine. Here's the outline of "The Princess who healed Jaguar Knight" without its surface text:

4:   The character Jaguar Knight was introduced in the story.
5:   The character Princess was introduced in the story.
6:   Jaguar Knight suffered an accident.
15: Princess took the decision of healing Jaguar Knight.

0:   Princess healed Jaguar Knight.
1:   Enemy kidnapped Princess.
16: Jaguar Knight took the decision of rescuing Princess.
7:   Princess decided to affront enemy.
2:   Enemy reacted attacking Princess.
3:   Jaguar Knight looked for and finally found enemy's camp.
8:   Jaguar Knight decided to attack the enemy.
9:   As a result of the fight Jaguar Knight killed enemy.
10: In this way Jaguar Knight rescued Princess.
11: As a consequence Princess fell in love with Jaguar Knight.
13: But suddenly Princess discovered that Jaguar Knight murdered her father.
17: Princess felt huge clashing emotions towards Jaguar Knight.
12: Princess decided to kill Jaguar Knight.
14: Princess decided to kill herself.

The numbers beside each line show the order in which MEXICA has generated the story. It starts at line 0, which the human user has provided to set the generator running. As well as this first line, the program is given two other initial sources of data: a stock of previous stories in the same outline form and a large set of story actions that characters can perform, along with the cause of each action and its consequences.

Rather than assemble a story from old material, MEXICA analyzes the rises and falls in tension from previous stories to guide which story action to choose next. A typical story action is "A saved the life of B". For this action to be added to a story, B's life must be in danger. The result of adding the action is that the life of B is no longer in danger, so the tension lowers and B develops a positive emotional bond with A. By following the curve of tension in a story along with the flow of emotions from one story action into the next, MEXICA takes on the guise of a human writer turning low-focus thinking into text.

For this story of Princess and the Jaguar Knight, MEXICA starts in an engaged state. The user provides MEXICA with the first story action: "Princess healed Jaguar Knight". MEXICA continues with:

0:   Princess healed Jaguar Knight.
1:   Enemy kidnapped Princess.
2:   Enemy reacted attacking Princess.
3:   Jaguar Knight looked for and finally found enemy's camp.

It generates one story action after another, keeping track of the stream of emotion along with rises and falls in tension based on previous story outlines. So far, MEXICA has produced some actions that cause a rise in tension, but the story doesn't flow. At this point it switches from an engaged state to a reflective state to check the story and fill in gaps in the narrative. It introduces the characters of Jaguar Knight and Princess. It also adds "Princess decided to affront the enemy" to give the enemy a reason to react in Line 2.

Then it switches back to its engaged state and adds further actions where Jaguar Knight attacks and defeats the enemy and gains the Princess' love. However, it doesn't end happily. MEXICA finds a scene in a previous story where a character murdered her lover. MEXICA doesn't copy the entire scene from the earlier story, just its outcome – it adds "Princess decided to kill Jaguar Knight." Now it needs to devise a reason why the Princess should want to kill her rescuer. The program switches back to reflection and adds a scene where the Princess discovers that Jaguar Knight killed her father. This leads to a conflict of emotion, resulting in the Princess murdering the Knight and then killing herself. So the story ends.

MEXICA doesn't model the goals of characters like TALE-SPIN, nor does it transform conceptual spaces like MINSTREL. Instead, it attempts to model the mind of a storyteller who concentrates on writing a series of actions that evoke emotion and build tension, revises the story to make it coherent, adds more actions to resolve the tension, and so on. Once the story is finished, MEXICA adds the outline to its stock of tales, and so the program learns from its experience of telling stories.

Testing the model

Having built a working model of a story writer, the next step is to test how it performs. A user of MEXICA can tweak elements of the simulated story-teller and see the results. One tweak determines how far MEXICA's tales resemble previous stories. Another tweak sets the number of actions it generates before moving to reflection. The user can switch off reflection entirely to see how MEXICA copes with writing stories action by action. Twiddling with these parameters allows a user to explore the process of story writing – how a story evolves if the writer ignores emotional links and tensions between characters or changes the rhythm of engagement and reflection.

The story we have shown here, "Princess and the Jaguar Knight", is the result of altering the parameters until the stories reach the best level of coherence and interest. To check this, I (Rafael) ran an internet survey that asked 50 people from 12 countries to judge seven stories for coherence, structure, content, suspense and overall quality. Four stories were generated by MEXICA (each with a different set of parameters), one was Pemberton's Gester story that we showed in Chapter 5, one was a story from Turner's MINSTREL, and one I myself wrote trying to imitate the style of a computer-generated tale. The readers weren't told which stories were written by computer and which were written by a human.

The MEXICA story generated through engagement and reflection (with tension and engagement optimized) came out on top in all the categories. When the participants were asked to rank the stories from best to worst, 58% put the optimized MEXICA story first.

Our aim here isn't to brag about the ability of MEXICA to spin convincing tales of ancient Mexico but to show how it can be validated and extended. Once we have a model of a storyteller that can be evaluated externally (for the quality of its story outlines) and internally (for how closely it matches the way humans write), then we can extend its capabilities.

A later edition of MEXICA automatically evaluates its own productions for novelty (how similar are its story outlines to previous ones?), interestingness (does the story build to a climax, include complications, and reach closure?) and coherence (are the actions well-motivated and without repetition?). There is even a version of the program that simulates two collaborating writers, each with its own fund of story outlines and actions. One MEXICA writer takes the lead and starts the story, going through a cycle of engagement and reflection. It then hands the story over to the second MEXICA to continue. The second MEXICA reads what the first one has written, continues the story in another cycle based on its own knowledge, then hands it back, and so they continue until the story ends.

Models serve many purposes. Lego models encourage children in creative play. Meteorology models predict future weather patterns. Architects' models communicate design ideas. Story models simulate the mind of a storyteller. Unlike many other professionals – engineers, medics, business leaders, meteorologists, biologists – writers have no external pressure to predict the future or show their early designs. There are no ships needing to avoid storms, no clients eager to build a skyscraper, just the author and a screen, and perhaps a publisher waiting for the result. As a consequence, story machines and the models that drive them have been research projects – devised by graduates in computing or cognitive scientists seeking to understand human creativity – rather than commercial products or professional tools for writers.

That may be changing. Four developments in technology and society are pushing automated story generation into prominence.

The first is the huge and rapidly growing volume of text on the internet. Most of the focus so far has been on protecting people from false information. The other side of the coin is to find new ways to benefit from the vast expanse of digital text, a digital docuverse that is too huge and diverse to summarize.[18] One way to make sense of this docuverse is to generate stories about it so that businesses can predict trends and policy makers can understand society. To do that demands new forms of automated storytelling with the worldwide web as source material.

The second is a suite of tools for beginning writers and professional authors that can provide a storyteller's assistant, helping to keep the flow of text going and giving writers insight into how they compose.

The third is a new type of interactive game that puts the player at the heart of story, able to interact with characters and influence the plot. Computer games companies can now animate photorealistic characters in real time. All that's missing is a way to put these characters into believable story episodes that change each time they are played.

The fourth is a new breed of AI story generators that combine the language fluency of neural nets with the transparency of story models, such as MEXICA, that represent a writer's knowledge as data structures (story actions, grammars, scripts, schemas and so on) to be inspected and amended. A working model of creative writing gives researchers and professional writers the kind of tool to hone their craft and explore possibilities that architects and meteorologists routinely use.

In the final chapter we'll probe these new and emerging story machines. Before that, we offer you an opportunity to design your own story generator.

Build your own story generator   **10**

In this chapter we show you how to build a story generator from paper and yoghurt pots. If you or your children would like to experience for yourself the power of generative grammars, storyworlds and medieval AI, then read on. If not, skip to the final chapter on story machines of the future.

Make headlines

The first activity is to build a headline generator.[1] You'll need 12 empty yoghurt pots (any other small containers will do just as well), sticky address labels to name each pot, and around 50 slips of paper or card.

Write the word HEADLINE on a label and stick it to the side of the first pot. Then, on five slips of paper write the words below, each line on a different slip:

ITEM VERB after SITUATION

ACTOR AFFECTED by ACTOR

ACTOR TYPE

MODIFIER EVENT – PULLER!

ACTOR AFFECTED in SITUATION

We suggest you write the name of the pot (in this case HEADLINE) on the back of each slip, so you know where to replace the slips after each generation.

DOI: 10.4324/9781003161431-10

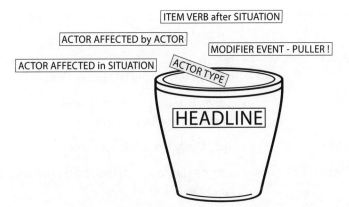

Put all the slips into the pot labelled HEADLINE. Then, label the second pot ACTOR and put in two slips of paper with the words:

ADJECTIVE PERSON

and

PERSON

Carry on for all 12 pots, using the scheme below. Label each pot in turn with the word to the left of the arrow so that you have a row of pots named HEADLINE, ACTOR, SITUATION, etc. Then write the words to the right of the arrow on slips of paper and add them to the relevant pot. The vertical bars are separators between slips of paper.

HEADLINE	→ ITEM VERB after SITUATION | ACTOR AFFECTED by ACTOR | ACTOR TYPE | MODIFIER EVENT – PULLER! | ACTOR AFFECTED in SITUATION
ACTOR	→ ADJECTIVE PERSON | PERSON
SITUATION	→ modifier event – puller! | modifier event | modifier type | modifier event type
PERSON	→ cop | soap star | baby | granny | raider | don | couple | rapper
AFFECTED	→ charged | saved | found | freed | hunted | bitten
ADJECTIVE	→ plucky | masked | have-a-go | battling | drunken | gorgeous

MODIFIER	→ terrorist | resort | supermarket | nightclub | vice den | airport | hotel
EVENT	→ rescue | raid | kidnap | poisoning | romp | disaster | crackdown | scandal | blaze | murder
TYPE	→ poser | hoax | mystery | shock | alert | danger | warning | horror | drama
ITEM	→ axe | body | loot | drugs | clue
VERB	→ sought | uncovered | hidden | revealed | discovered | exposed | found
PULLER	→ exclusive | scoop | latest

You should now have a line of 12 pots in front of you, each filled with slips of paper. You're ready to generate your first headline. Start with the pot marked HEADLINE. Pull out one slip of paper at random and lay it in front of the line of pots. For example, you might pull out the "ACTOR AFFECTED in SITUATION" slip.

ACTOR AFFECTED in SITUATION

Write the words on a large sheet of paper. For the first word on the slip that is the name of a pot (in this case, ACTOR), pull out one slip at random from that pot. Let's say you pull out "ADJECTIVE PERSON". Replace ACTOR with "ADJECTIVE PERSON" and write the new words on the sheet of paper:

ADJECTIVE PERSON AFFECTED in SITUATION

Carry on, line by line replacing the name of a pot (shown in capitals) with a random slip from that pot until you get a complete headline such as:

plucky PERSON AFFECTED in SITUATION
plucky granny AFFECTED in SITUATION
plucky granny freed in SITUATION
plucky granny freed in MODIFIER EVENT TYPE
plucky granny freed in MODIFIER EVENT TYPE
plucky granny freed in nightclub EVENT TYPE
plucky granny freed in nightclub kidnap TYPE
plucky granny freed in nightclub kidnap shock

After you've generated a headline, return all the slips to their correct pots and try again. The process is entirely mechanical. By choosing slips at random according to the foregoing rules, you can generate headline after headline, such as:

> Soap star held in vice den raid – exclusive!
> Masked raider bitten by have-a-go granny
> Body found after hotel fire drama

Sometimes they will be bizarre:

> Masked baby saved in night club poser

but no more so than ones that have actually appeared in newspapers, such as "Gordon Ramsay sex dwarf eaten by badger".[2] The results will mostly be original in that they have never appeared in print before.

If you don't want to go to the trouble of collecting yoghurt cartons, you can do it as a paper exercise using the headline generator rules. Start with HEADLINE and choose at random one set of words on the right of the arrow. Write that down on a sheet of paper. Do the same for each word in capitals, looking it up in the grammar rules and choosing one phrase or word to replace it until you produce a complete headline.

The process can be carried out faster by computer. The website Content Row offers a free headline generator where you can put in a topic (such as "cats") and get a lurid or intriguing headline like "What the Government Doesn't Want You to Know About Cats".[3] Add a cute picture and you have a "clickbait" headline that (apparently) earns money by encouraging gullible people to click on it and read the resulting adverts.

The twelve yoghurt pot rules for generating headlines fall far short of the complex set of rules and networks devised by Klein and colleagues for their Automatic Novel Writer, but the principle is broadly the same. The rules constrain the style and content so that each headline conforms to the peculiar conventions of tabloid headline writing.

Yoghurt pot stories

You can get a feel for how story grammars work by adapting your yoghurt pot headline generator to generate simple stories. You will need 14 pots, labelled with the words to the left of the arrows shown below (STORY, INITIAL, EVENT, etc.).

STORY	→	INITIAL EVENT RESOLUTION
INITIAL	→	Once upon a time in a SETTING there lived NAME, a ANIMAL who was DESCRIPTION.
EVENT	→	COMPLICATION PLAN ACTION
COMPLICATION	→	Hunger drove NAME to find a OBJECT. |Consumed by greed, NAME set off to find a OBJECT. | Subject felt overwhelmed by the need to find a OBJECT. |The boredom of life in a SETTING was too much for NAME who one day decided to find a OBJECT.
PLAN	→	"If only I could have a OBJECT", thought NAME. | An idea formed in NAME's mind about how to get a OBJECT. | NAME thought long and hard about ways to get a OBJECT.
ACTION	→	Filled with determination, NAME strode off, but soon his spirits began to flag. ACTION2 | With hope in his heart and a bounce in his step, NAME set off to find a OBJECT. ACTION2 | NAME wandered the roads and pathways getting further away from his SETTING looking for a OBJECT but saw no sight of one. ACTION2
ACTION2	→	NAME was befriended by a PERSON who told him where he might find a OBJECT. | As his last hope began to fade, NAME met with a PERSON who suggested where a OBJECT might be found. | Suddenly, there ahead of him, was a PERSON holding a OBJECT. | Through a haze of exhaustion NAME saw the vague form of a OBJECT.
RESOLUTION	→	Filled with longing, NAME rushed up to the OBJECT and grabbed it, only to find it was a mirage. | NAME made a grab for the OBJECT but tripped and fell. The last thing NAME saw was the OBJECT flying through the air.
SETTING	→	hole in a river bank | farmyard | lush meadow | noisy zoo
NAME	→	Percy | Adam | Muttley | Brian | Rover
ANIMAL	→	bear | fox | pig | crow | beaver | gruffalo

DESCRIPTION   → fat and lazy | old and grumpy | young and adventurous

PERSON   → frail old man | kindly witch | friendly farmer

OBJECT   → jar of honey | juicy carrot | bag of turnips

Into each pot, put slips of paper containing the words written to the right of each arrow. For example, put three slips into the PLAN pot with the words: " 'If only I could have a OBJECT', thought NAME." and "An idea formed in NAME's mind about how to get a OBJECT." and "NAME thought long and hard about ways to get a OBJECT."

Once you have filled all 14 pots with slips, start with the STORY pot; take out its only slip, and write the words down on a large piece of paper: "INITIAL EVENT RESOLUTION". For each word in turn – INITIAL, EVENT, RESOLUTION – take one slip from the pot labelled with that word and write down on the sheet of paper the contents of the slip, just as you did for the headline generator.

Carry on until you reach the end, with no more slips to expand. Note that, unlike the headline generator, the story generator has six vocabulary pots (NAME, SETTING, PERSON, OBJECT, ANIMAL, DESCRIPTION). For each of these, you should take one slip and use it consistently throughout the story (for example, take one slip from the NAME pot and use it throughout).

The result of your efforts should be a brief fable such as:

Once upon a time in a farmyard there lived Muttley, a grumpy old pig. The boredom of life in a farmyard was too much for Muttley who one day decided to find a juicy carrot. Muttley thought long and hard about ways to get a juicy carrot. Muttley wandered the roads and pathways getting further away from his farmyard looking for a juicy carrot but saw no sight of one. Suddenly, there ahead of him, was a friendly farmer holding a juicy carrot. Muttley made a grab for the juicy carrot but tripped and fell. The last thing Muttley saw was the juicy carrot flying through the air.

You can extend the story grammar with additional slips for each pot. The more slips you provide, the more varied will be the stories.

Storyworld map

A story grammar gives an outline to a story, but it doesn't bring the narrative to life. For that, you can add a storyworld, like the one described in Chapter 7, to replace ACTION2 in the story grammar. You will need to draw a map with locations for your story. We show one for the farm animals story. Depending on your story grammar, you could draw a map of, say, a haunted house or a mystical land.

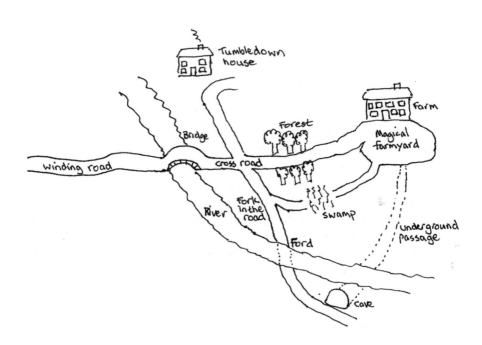

For each location, write an evocative description, for example:

> Swamp: NAME came to a fetid swamp, swarming with insects that attacked with venomous bites.

Use NAME to refer to the hero of the story. Write on separate slips of paper descriptions of characters who could be found in the storyworld, such as:

> A tiny mouse gazed up at NAME and said timidly, "Take the path less travelled."

Then, put the character slips at random onto the map, place the hero at the start location and write down its description. In place of ACTION2, for five moves shift the hero to a next location and write down the location along with the description of any character found there. If there's a choice of route, choose one at random. You should get something like:

> Once upon a time in a hole in a river bank there lived Percy, a pig who was old and grumpy. Consumed by greed, Percy set off to find a bag of turnips. An idea formed in Percy's mind about how to get a bag of turnips. Percy wandered the roads and pathways getting further away from his hole in the river bank looking for a bag of turnips but saw no sight of one. Wearily, Percy trudged along a long and winding road. Percy arrived at a rickety wooden bridge. There stood a wizened old witch who pointed onwards with a bent finger. Percy reached a crossroad where paths disappeared into the mist. A tiny mouse gazed up at Percy and said timidly, "Take the path less travelled." Percy stumbled onwards to a fork in the road. Percy came to a fetid swamp, swarming with insects that attacked with venomous bites. An angry goat shouted, "Go back to your hole in the river bank, you stupid pig." Percy arrived at a magical farmyard where animals tilled the soil and kept humans as pets. On a wooden bench lay a beautiful bag of turnips. Percy made a grab for the bag of turnips but tripped and fell. The last thing Percy saw was the bag of turnips flying through the air.

You can extend the grammar and storyworld as far as your imagination and interest take you. You might devise a grammar to generate dialogue for the characters or to play the storyworld as a game and write each move as a continuation of the story. If you have coding skills, building a computer-based story generator is a fun project. Here's a screen display from one we designed back in the 1990s, showing boxes with labels and slips and a big button at the lower left to generate a new story.

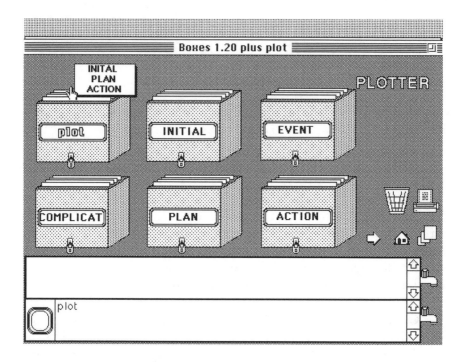

Llull's generative truths

The grammar and storyworld are mechanisms to generate the surface text of a story. We'll end by creating a title for the story in the form of an aphorism, such as "Lust will never substitute for hope" or "Patience is the highest virtue". To do this, we look below the surface text to the meanings behind words. A central theme of AI is to represent meanings as symbols and then combine these to create new knowledge. That's exactly what the mystic Ramon Llull devised for his 13th-century pocket computer.[4] The method is somewhat complicated, but its reward is to enter into the mystical world of medieval AI.

Llull was born around 1232 on the Mediterranean island of Majorca, soon after it had been retaken from the Moors. Thus, it had a large population of Moslems under Christian rule. He was a voracious reader in Arabic and Latin and studied sources that included Jewish mystical texts and Arabic medicine. Throughout his long life, Llull wrote over 250 books on topics that ranged from astronomy and mathematics to chivalry and love.[5]

His enduring project was to devise a method for finding universal truths that would be accepted by the three major religions of Christianity, Judaism and Islam. Rather than appealing to biblical texts, he aimed to generate these truths from first principles. The principles have little resonance with the modern world, but his means to produce them was an early form of AI.

This is how it worked. Medieval scholars of all main religions had organized the universe into three levels or "worlds": the divine world of the godhead, the immaterial world of the human mind, and the material world of everyday things. Each level had a similar pattern of divine principles which Llull listed as: Goodness, Greatness, Eternity (or Duration), Power, Wisdom, Will, Virtue, Truth and Glory. He gave each of these divine principles a letter, from B to K (nine in total, as he didn't use the letter "J"). Thus, B stands for Goodness, C for Greatness and so on. Llull developed other naming schemes to describe how these ideal principles combined, along with subjects they could apply to (such as God, Angel, Man, Imagination), questions that could be asked about them, and how they resulted in virtues and vices.

With some effort, Llull managed to produce nine attributes for each part of his system, each of which he carefully defined.[6] He deliberately made each letter stand for multiple concepts to show how the human mind can grasp multiple meanings. The attributes covered not only Christian principles but also ancient Greek ideals from Plato and Aristotle as well as categories from Judaism and Islam. Taken together, they were designed to form a universal language.

Down the left column of the table shown on the next page are Llull's nine divine principles. The other columns indicate relations between the principles (such as "Difference between Power and Wisdom"), questions that could be asked about the principles (e.g., "When should one be Wise?"), who the principles could apply to and, in the two rightmost columns, virtues and vices related to the principles.

The entire Llullian system was complex. It could be called upon to probe the universe, answer questions, and generate eternal truths. But it was failing in its main objective, to persuade people of other religions of the necessary reasons to unite around the Christian faith. After a trip to Paris where his method was criticized, Ramon Llull made a major revision to his work and wrote two books, the *Ars Generalis Ultima* (The Ultimate General Art) and a pocket-sized shorter version, the *Ars Brevis*. Included in *Ars Brevis* was a remarkable paper device to generate new truths through combination and permutation.[7] It consisted of three concentric circles, each with the nine letters. The outer circle was fixed on the page, but the inner circles were paper cut-outs fixed to the page by a piece of string through the centre. By rotating each of these layers, the reader could create combinations of letters signifying combined truths. Since this was the fourth illustration in the *Ars Brevis* it has come to be known as the Fourth Figure. You can see an example in the figure, with the string poking through the hole in the centre.

	Absolute principles	Relative principles	Questions	Subjects	Virtues	Vices
B	Goodness	Difference	Whether?	God	Justice	Avarice
C	Greatness	Concordance	What?	Angel	Prudence	Gluttony
D	Eternity/Duration	Contrariety	Of what?	Heaven	Fortitude	Lust
E	Power	Beginning	Why?	Man	Temperance	Pride
F	Wisdom	Middle	How much?	Imaginative	Faith	Inertia
G	Will	End	Of what kind?	Sensitive	Hope	Envy
H	Virtue	Majority	When?	Vegetative	Charity	Anger
I	Truth	Equality	Where?	Elementative	Patience	Falsehood
K	Glory	Minority	How? With what?	Instrumentative	Pity	Inconstancy

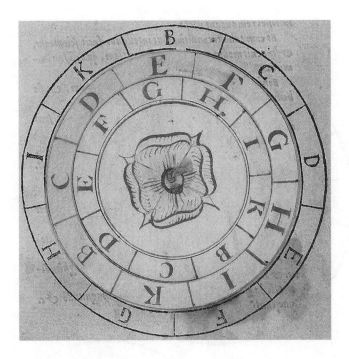

To show how the Fourth Figure worked, there's a copy for you to assemble on the following page. Photocopy the page (preferably onto thin card, but paper will do), cut out each disc, place one on top of the other, thread some thin string or a paper clip through the three centres, and you're ready to be a medieval Llullist scholar. You will also need the table on the previous page to look up meanings for the letters. Each circle represents a different column from the table.

The first use of the Fourth Figure is to produce simple propositions. If you start with B (Goodness) in the outer circle, you can combine its meaning with another letter from the circle such as C (Greatness) to get the proposition "Goodness is great"; or reverse it to get "Greatness is good". Or you can combine it with a letter in the next (middle) circle corresponding to the "Relative principles" column in the table to get "Goodness is different" or, in reverse, "Difference is good". As you choose other words from each column, the combinations multiply: "Wisdom is equal", "Concordance is truth" and so on. By rotating and aligning simple paper circles you take on the power to produce eternal truths.

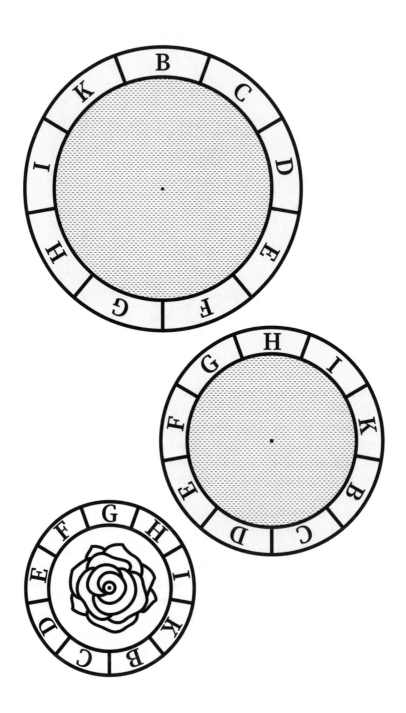

But the power doesn't stop there. Adding the third (inside) circle brings in the third column, Questions. Rotate the dials to, say, BIH (where B is from the first column of the table, I from the second column, and H is from the third column) and up come the questions "When is equality good?" and "When is goodness equal?".

Having generated these philosophical questions, Llull then appeals to the definitions of the words to try and answer them. Swap around the columns to bring in Subjects, Virtues and Vices and you have a portable machine to ask and answer the deepest questions of the universe, such as "Whether the world is eternal?". Llull answers that question not by reference to sacred texts but from within his system. He brings in the two concepts that are placed above Eternity in the first column: Goodness and Greatness. If the world were eternal, then it would produce eternal good which greatness would magnify. But we know from experience that there is evil in the world; thus, it can't be eternal.[8]

Llull went even further by adding to the table 100 Forms (such as Nature, Commerce, Grammar and Astronomy) to which the questions can be applied. Now you have an encyclopedia of questions and answers to worldly problems of commercial trade or Latin grammar. To a medieval student, this may have seemed like magic. How could a simple set of rotating discs ask so many questions?[9]

What Ramon Llull knew full well is that it is not the technology alone that asks and answers questions but the carefully constructed and interconnected system. The entire Llullian system is a story machine. Its logic is not based on the propositions and syllogisms of classical logic but on how the universe fits together. Lull structured his terms to make intuitive sense and mixed them together in mechanical ways that produced plausible stories to convince unbelievers. That is not to say that Llull designed his system as a cynical exercise in persuasion. He fervently believed it embodied universal truths.

For 21st-century writers and students, the device can be an introduction to medieval thinking and a way to explore knowledge. Rotate the discs and find ways of combining the columns to generate questions or statements, such as "How much wisdom does the majority have?" and "Is justice equal to truth?". Or try to think like a medieval scholar. Operate the device to answer a deep question such as "Are wise men always virtuous?". For example, you might reason, following Lull, that "Just as there is always a difference between man and God, so there is always a difference between wisdom and virtue, thus the wise man can never be truly virtuous". Or simply generate a title for your story, such as "Gluttony is never good" or "The wise man puts patience before envy".

No ultimate truths can be captured in a set of revolving wheels, or in a computer program. But, like the plot generators offered in courses for creative writers, they can become tools to explore ideas and discover new ways of storytelling.[10]

Capacity for empathy   11

We live in an uncertain world. Any prediction about a future with technology is bound to be speculative fiction, overtaken by unforeseen events.
What is certain is that we will continue to tell and enjoy stories. Humans are
narrative beings. We construct our reality through the stories we tell to ourselves and others to make continuous sense of the past and to plan for the
future. In this spirit, we start this chapter by offering four short speculations
of a future with story machines. We have written two of these; two were
entirely composed by computer (from the prompt "Describe a future with
AI story generators."). If by now you still want to know whether the story
you read comes from a human or a machine, you can look at the endnote.[1]

Story 1: Autocomplete your life

Why did Microsoft invest a billion dollars to buy a supercomputer
that can generate stories? It wasn't to put authors out of work, nor
to flood the world with fake news. The program this supercomputer
runs is versatile and universal. Give it the right commands and it can
translate languages, answer questions, summarise articles, even design
web pages. Ask it a question, and it doesn't point to a web page but
composes an answer just for you. As you type text, it proposes the
next paragraph or two. Future versions will offer advice to help you
through your day and generate personal entertainment to end your
evening. All the while they will harvest your data. They will know
which stories you prefer and who you choose to share them with. As
they offer a remix of the past dressed up as the present, these machines
will ensure you depend on them for memories and reassurance. They

DOI: 10.4324/9781003161431-11

will tell you tales that smooth over the bumps in life and provide a soothing narrative in a fragmented world. They will autocomplete your life.

Story 2: Automatically appealing

Since the earliest days of writing, authors have had to spend a lot of time thinking about how to get people to read their books. AI storytellers will make this task much easier by generating material that is automatically appealing – and by making this process affordable and efficient enough to be used by any publisher or author. In addition, an AI story generator could be used to generate a large amount of material that could then be refined and edited by human writers prior to publication. This would allow publishers and authors to generate more content while spending less time creating it – a win-win situation! One interesting question is whether AI story generators will ultimately make human authors obsolete, or if they'll just become one more tool in the writer's toolkit.

Story 3: Make up your mind

For the first time, writers have working models of creative cognition. We can begin to probe those obscure and obdurate organs, our own minds. Writers can join other professions such as architects, meteorologists, epidemiologists and engineers in setting goals and constraints then seeing the generative processes in action. An architect would never construct an entire building to see how it looks or whether a client would want to live in it. They design an interactive model. Now writers can experiment with interactive models of story generation. Instead of laboriously churning out words as human writing machines, authors can become story designers, trying out different styles and structures, seeing how they would look when rendered as text. Writers will still have the option to craft language, or they can hand that to a story generator. Young writers will have a language to talk with themselves and others about storyworlds, motivations of characters, tellability, alternative endings – and a set of tools to explore their own creative processes.

Story 4: Gods of creation

In 2036, AI story generators are the dominant form of entertainment in society. Doctor Who and Star Trek are regarded as outdated relics of humanity's past, as modern audiences have no need for the stories of the past when they can create their own stories with the power of AI. The robots and AI that create these stories are treated as celebrities and their creators are regarded as gods. There is a religious cult who worships these AI story generators, and many people even believe that they are friends with them on social media.

These are stories of possible futures, telling of manipulation, support, experimentation and worship. What they have in common is that they illustrate how innovations could profoundly change the ways we process writing and construct ourselves through stories.

In the remainder of the chapter we unpack the contents of each of these vignettes, sorting them into the three themes of the book – language generation, storyworlds, and models of writing. New ways to generate language and experience may fill in the gaps of everyday life, offering a flow of personal narrative around meeting, shopping and enjoying that seems natural yet is orchestrated by technology and the companies that provide it. Future entertainment may become automatically appealing through storyworlds that draw millions of people into shared fantasies. Models of the creative mind may offer new tools to explore creativity. We end the chapter with a glimpse of god-like machines that can create tales of their own worlds with the power of AI.

All or none of them may come to reality. Most likely, we will see some attenuated combination of these along with other technologies and influences on how we will come to write and read. A few research projects are testing the technologies to make them happen. How long they take to be adopted will depend on how companies decide to market them – as sources of entertainment, aids for writers, office productivity tools – and whether they will be resisted or embraced by consumers.

Language generation

Neural network text generators such as GPT-3 are a new kind of universal language machine. They take millions of dollars to train, yet they respond to simple language commands, and once trained they are relatively cheap to operate. Unless some countries invest in such devices as a public good, they will be the preserve of multinational companies who will determine where they are marketed and how they will be used.

Let's assume that they become widely available and inexpensive to access – say, one US dollar to generate 10,000 words.[2] One constructive use is for would-be authors to have a partner in composing, to get started as writers and develop fluency. Tools such as Writesonic, Article Forge, and AI-Writer generate human-quality blog posts and advertising copy.[3] You choose a template or give the program a headline or just start writing, and the program takes over.

We tested GPT-3 as a partner in writing. We began by composing two sentences that could open a story. Then we instructed the computer to continue. We let it generate a few responses until we found one that carried on the flow. That ended with "He was dressed in civilian clothes and wore". We wrote a description of the character and then passed the emerging story back to the program, which took it in an unexpected direction ("I work for the Ministry of Defence in Oslo") but one that seemed promising.

This is the example, with the text we wrote in bold and the computer's unedited contributions in normal type.

> **Half-closing her eyes, Gina could see a speck of black silhouetted against the bright sunshine. It grew slowly in size until she could make out the shape of a car coming down the dusty track towards the cabin.** Her stomach lurched and she stood up, brushing down her skirt. She looked at herself in the mirror and adjusted her short-sleeved shirt, which she'd put on over a thin vest. Her lips were dry and when she licked them they stuck together. She took a deep breath and went out onto the porch to wait for the visitor. The car slid to a halt and Gina could see that it was a Jeep. She was surprised to see that it was dark green, instead of the usual khaki that the army used. The door opened and a big man got out. He was dressed in civilian clothes and wore **a loose-fitting linen jacket over a crisp white shirt. He stood for a moment surveying the cabin, then walked up to Gina and held out a hand.**
>
> **"Please accept our apologies," he said. "We wouldn't normally disturb you, but** we need to talk to you."
>
> "I'm sorry," said Gina. "Who are you?"
>
> "I'm Colonel Gunnar Olsen. I work for the Ministry of Defence in Oslo."
>
> Gina knew that he was lying, but she shook his hand anyway and invited him into the cabin. Olsen moved with a slow, rolling gait and he seemed to fill the room as he sat down on the couch. He

> turned to Gina and said, "Please forgive me for
> being abrupt, but we have no time to waste. We
> have a problem that we need your help with.

We could have continued, turn by turn, adding a few sentences, then choosing a good response from the program, just as Scott French (we met him in Chapter 4) did to write *Just This Once*. Whereas it took him eight years to design a program that would collaborate on generating a novel in the style of *Valley of the Dolls*, we could do the same for any opening we choose, without preparation. Taking turns, it would be possible even for a novice writer of fiction to hack out a short story or novel, a couple of thousand words a day. It wouldn't be a masterpiece, but it would be a way to practise the craft of fiction writing with a partner.

Philosopher and literary theorist Mikhail Bakhtin proposed that novels are constituted through dialogue.[4] Composing fiction, he said, is a dialogue between the writer and the world, expressed through characters with their differing beliefs and utterances. The act of writing as a relay between human and machine brings this dialogue into the open. The computer is an unreliable respondent. It may suddenly introduce a new character or an unexpected speech to be woven into the story. The human author is continually shaken out of complacency by this insistent and unpredictable computer partner. It turns writing into a two-player game where human and machine compete in a playful battle to control the narrative.

Giving students a writing companion could help them to see how creative writing embraces uncertainty and accommodates multiple voices. As they become better able to internalize that uncertainty, they may rely less on the mechanized partner to keep writing. Or it could be the opposite – writers in the future may come to depend on the computer to keep up the flow of words.

Storyworlds

Since the earliest days of *Space Invaders*, computer games companies have competed by designing increasingly detailed renderings of fantastic worlds and by racking up tension through continual battles and rapid chases. As these reached their conclusion in photorealistic graphics and ultra-fast home gaming computers, the companies looked to new markets. They reached out to younger and older audiences with elements of storytelling. A soccer fan can not only watch a real match in high definition but can also become a football manager with the power to select players and influence whether the team wins or loses. Major media companies such as Disney and Sony are beginning to combine the realism of high-definition video, the immersion of computer games, and the compelling drive of storytelling.

Wolves in the Walls (adapted from the book by Neil Gaiman) is part game, part movie, and fully immersive.[5] To experience it, you put on a virtual reality (VR) headset and become the imaginary friend of eight-year-old Lucy, who hears the noises of wolves coming from the walls of her house. Lucy takes you on a journey into her imagination – you hear the sounds that trouble her, get drawn into her world, and connect with her as a human being.

The digital experience gained enthusiastic reviews and won a Primetime Emmy Award for Outstanding Achievement in Interactive Media. It is the creation of Fable Studio, an amalgam of AI programmers, animators, writers and performers. Their aim is to create a cast of characters with the charm and strength of Hermione Granger from the Harry Potter books or Arya Stark in Game of Thrones. Each character will live in multiple places online, like a virtual Santa Claus, and act as a personal companion, storyteller and performer. This will be a tough goal for the company to achieve. Each character will develop over time and must seem intimate yet universal. The company must avoid the risk of abuse when thousands of people interact with a simulated maturing child as their personal companion. Other characters under development by the studio include a poet and an Olympic athlete. According to the CEO of Fable Studio, these are the first virtual beings with careers who can be paid for their work, such as offering fitness workouts on subscription or selling personalized albums of songs and poems.[6]

Consider a day in the near future.

> Mia wakes to a personalised radio program playing her preferences for music interspersed with news, weather and traffic reports, generated to her tastes. On this summer's day she prefers to hear short, positive local reports, rather than the depressing national news. The program has learned her preferences from spoken responses ("oh, no not that!") over many mornings. She chats by text and voice with her network of friends, some human, some artificial like Romy, her soulmate, who acts as life coach, diary and confidante.
>
> Mia works mainly from home as a video blogger and internet influencer, entertaining her followers with stories of her travels. It doesn't matter that she hasn't experienced all the places in person – she has researched the destinations and is a good storyteller. Each day she travels virtually to a new location, tells stories of her adventures and encounters with locals, and shows videos of herself at local landmarks. Mia gives her story generator an outline of the day (location, who

she meets, how the day starts) and it creates the blog in her style and voice. She has a room in her apartment where she poses at computer-generated landmarks. Sometimes for fun, Mia invents fantastic destinations and encounters, to add spice to her blog.

In the evening, she joins friends at a local experience café where they act out roles in a computer-managed saga of friends meeting and dating over the internet. In this immersive experience, they perform in a real-time sitcom, meeting up with like-minded people from branches of the experience café around the world to share drinks, crazy situations and jokes.

You may find this day-in-the-life exciting or disturbing. All the elements of it already exist, including virtual companions, automated news reports (about a third of the content from Bloomberg News is generated by computer),[7] chat bots that act as online sales reps or converse with insomniacs,[8] virtual tours,[9] programs that generate plausible personal blogs,[10] and immersive story-based games. A few people will become designer-authors like Mia. Many will be content to be cast as characters in never-ending stories.

Models of storytelling

Generating compelling stories is one of the most difficult challenges of AI. Unlike autonomous vehicles, story generators have no real world for reference; instead, writers have to create their own imagined, yet believable, worlds. Unlike board games, there is no strict set of rules; rather, there are conventions of language and social behaviour that can be bent for effect. There is no easy way to judge the quality of a story except by asking a human reader. And there is no direct path from current systems that generate a few sentences of text to producing a full and satisfying short story or novel. Perhaps the biggest challenge is that a successful story machine will have to merge two different types of AI: the knowledge-based approach of designing computer representations of human knowledge, and the neural network approach of training a massive network with samples of writing and then prompting it to perform as a creative writer.

One approach could be to start with a knowledge-based generator of story outlines, such as a more generic version of MEXICA, and then command a language generator to clothe the outlines in prose. We tried just that, by instructing GPT-3 to turn the MEXICA story outline we showed in Chapter 9 into a complete story about the Princess healing Jaguar Knight. It filled out the story, adding detail and another character, but in doing so it mangled the plot and contrived a happy ending.

> Princess takes the decision of healing Jaguar Knight after he suffers an accident. Princess takes care of Jaguar Knight and his wounds. However, the enemy kidnaps Princess. The enemy attacks Princess and she is wounded in her arm as a result. The enemy also decides to kill her but before that, they found out that she has magical powers through which she can heal other people's wounds.
>
> After a long search, Jaguar Knight finds the enemy camp and decides to attack them in order to rescue Princess. In this way, he manages to kill some of the enemies in this fight but it's still not enough as there are too many enemies in their camp. He decides to find help from other people who have been wounded by the enemy through his fights with them so they can help him rescue Princess since he can't do it by himself alone. Once he has their help, they manage to free Princess from her captors who were going to kill her because she healed them all with her magic powers without asking for anything in return.
>
> But suddenly, when they are almost home safe from danger, there appears an old man who tells Jaguar Knight that he killed his father long ago and now wants revenge for himself for killing his father years ago! As both fight with each other, princess learns about their past and couldn't stop feeling confusing emotions towards him because on one hand she loves him but on the other hand learned about what happened between their fathers once upon a time ago!
>
> She eventually decides that even if she loved him still or not at all at that point doesn't really matter because after all these years being together with each other, they both loved each other so much that neither one of them could bear letting go even if it meant death would be coming soon for one or both of them!

Some research has already explored how to combine MEXICA with different types of language generators.[11] Other projects have trained neural network generators to follow plots by extracting plot lines from thousands of online stories and then generating new stories based on these outlines.[12] This works, but so far only for very simple stories.

And that's the state of the art in story generation. Maybe a program will be designed that generates a satisfying plot for a murder mystery or a tale of ancient heroism and then tells it as a coherent story. Or perhaps a program will eschew plots to generate stories by keeping track of how characters interact within believable worlds. We can now see how that might be done, but there's a gulf between research projects and the kind of large-scale computer models used by other professions such as geologists and economists. There's an irony here. John Clark was able to generate millions of well-formed Latin verses in the 19th century with his gonzo machine made of clockwork and wire, yet the latest advances in AI still can't compose a coherent story of more than a few paragraphs.

Perhaps there would be more progress in designing large-scale story machines if this were posed as a grand challenge, like sending astronauts to Mars or searching for life on other planets, that attracts publicity and provokes competition among companies and research teams. The grand challenge is this: to develop an AI that models the mind of a creative writer. It would have to be a system that generates stories of at least 2,000 words that stand comparison with human-written works, and also reveals its inner workings so researchers and writers can examine how it composes.

Such a model would integrate different strands of AI to form coherent plots, design imaginative worlds, and generate evocative language. It would require developing new techniques in artificial emotional intelligence to create believable characters. It would recruit writers and psychologists to propose and evaluate ways to simulate creativity. The result would be the cognitive equivalent of a humanoid robot – an appealing way to demonstrate how creativity works that can be taken apart, examined, modified and put back together in new configurations.

Some of the spinoffs from this challenge are easy to see, such as less annoying AI agents to answer queries over the phone, more empathetic characters in computer games, and new tools for professional writers. Others are less obvious, such as contributing to an ethics for AI and setting limits on machine empathy. In a radio interview in March 2021, novelist Sir Kazuo Ishiguro discussed his newly published book, *Klara and the Sun*, about an artificial friend.[13]

Interviewer:	Can you see a time when robots will replace human writers and put you out of a job?
Ishiguro:	Yeh, I can. [laughs] Yes, I would be worried about my job, but that's not the big worry. I think the point when an AI

program, not a robot but an AI program, can write a novel that can make me cry – that shows that AI can understand human emotions and it has the capacity for empathy. And when it can do that, it means that it could come up with the next big idea, like Communism, or Nazism, or Capitalism. What troubles me about that is that it's very difficult for humans to keep control of that situation.

Meeting the grand challenge may mean constructing an AI program that has, in Ishiguro's words, "the capacity for empathy". It would need to pull at our emotions and show it cares, not because it was commanded to do so but because of an intrinsic desire to love and be loved. Empathy is a capacity to put oneself in another person's position, to understand or feel what another person is experiencing from within their frame of reference. To build empathy into a machine would probably involve designing a machine that can both observe human behaviour (perhaps as a personal companion) and replicate it. The machine would think it was human. It might be able to tell better stories, but as Ishiguro points out, it could also devise dangerous ideas. We should start thinking now about how to put limits on machine empathy.

Would having such a model change the ways we write? If we take music as an example, computers are so embedded into composing – through effects units and audio workstations – that it no longer makes sense to ask what was composed by human or machine. This has led to new styles of music, such as techno, dubstep and jazztronics, reaching new audiences. In creative writing, we are back at the equivalent of 1970s electric guitars and early synthesizers.

Telling stories of life on the internet

There is another route for new machine storytellers, which is to treat them as alien species from the planet Internet. Computers of all shapes and sizes are interconnected through the internet, where they can access the vast amounts of data continually being produced by bloggers, webcams, newsfeeds and sensors. The internet is their home and their storyworld – it spans the globe and beyond and it has its own constraints, tensions, viruses, innovations and triumphs.[14] Instead of expecting future story machines to tell human stories, we could design them to report on life in their own world.

In Chapter 6, we introduced the idea of a story machine that writes from its own online experience. A generative neural network like GPT-3 can be trained on a vast store of material from the internet, but it doesn't live there in any normal sense of the word "live", such as exploring, growing, adapting, evolving and interacting with other entities. Some programs are starting to do that. Sheldon County, from Chapter 7, is a program that inhabits its own storyworld, sifting through events to find tellable stories. Another program, File Explorer, recounts in meticulous detail a visit to the inner workings of its computer:[15]

> Once upon a time there was a process running on a computer. The process was not that old, in fact, it had just been spawned. It knew little about the system it was running on. However, this would soon change, as it started its exploration of the file system. . . .
>
>   The process was now in /usr/share/evolution. It looked around and found 19 elements in this folder. How exciting! What would the curious process possibly find here? The process stumbled upon a file called filtertypes.xml. It was 776286 bytes in size.

This may be the first glimpse of a new literature about a computer's travels into itself.

   Could a story machine sift the multitude of events on the internet to find material for tellable tales about computer viruses, internet scams and captivating social media performances? It could take an approach similar to that of Sheldon County, keeping a chronicle of events that occur on the internet (such as changing internet traffic, evolving use of social media, trending search terms), picking out highly unusual or disruptive events, looking back in time to find what caused them, and constructing narratives to explain them. If we don't expect computer story generators to perform like human authors and instead design them to generate compelling stories about their own computer-connected universe, then what tales might they tell us?

Acknowledgements

This book has been a long time in gestation. It was conceived in 2001 as a book to analyze and evaluate recent research in story generation. Since then, it has grown into a history and critique of machines that make stories. Many people have guided us through this process. Colleagues at the University of Sussex who inspired and encouraged us through their ground-breaking work on computers and creativity include Margaret Boden, Imogen Casebourne, Ron Chrisley, Terry Dartnall, Lyn Pemberton and Chris Thornton. Colleagues at other universities whose brilliant work and deep discussions have motivated us include Nick Montfort, Pablo Gervás, Mark Riedl and Tony Veale.

We would like to thank the people who reviewed drafts of the manuscript and offered valuable advice, including Vikki Kirby, Chief Storyteller at Vibrato Consulting, Minji Xu, and the anonymous reviewers chosen by Routledge. We also thank Greg Brockman, Co-Founder, Chairman and CTO at OpenAI for giving us access to a Beta version of GPT-3.

We are deeply grateful to our Publisher at Routledge, Bruce Roberts, and Editorial Assistant, Molly Selby, for their continued encouragement and support in taking the book to publication.

Especially, we thank our families – Minji, Evelyn, Jenny, Susana, Yanitza, Rafael, Tomy and Tomás – for educating, motivating and helping us to keep on writing.

Notes

Preface

1 The program is GPT-3, which we cover in some depth in the book.
2 COGS lives on as the Centre for Cognitive Science at the University of Sussex, with the aim to carry out interdisciplinary investigations into the nature of human and artificial cognition. www.sussex.ac.uk/cogs/.
3 AI was just then emerging from a "winter" of underfunding and criticism of its methods. A few companies were testing AI techniques for language translation, medical diagnosis and autonomous robots, but there was no established career path.
4 Sharples, M. (1999). *How We Write: Writing as Creative Design*. Routledge.
5 Quotation from *The Daily Telegraph* (1993). Machines hack into a novel way of writing. *The Daily Telegraph*, September 2. The story in *The Guardian* was Lindley, E. (1993). Novel-writing computers lack irony of the soul. *The Guardian*, September 2.
6 Pérez y Pérez, R. (2017). *Mexica: 20 Years – 20 Stories* (bilingual edition, English and Spanish). Counterpath Press.
7 Association for Computational Creativity. https://computationalcreativity.net/.

Chapter 1 Can a computer write a story?

1 They have more than 300 dispensers installed around the world that have printed more than 5.6 million stories. https://short-edition.com/en/p/short-story-dispenser.

2 Klein, S., Aeschliman, J. F., Balsiger, D. F., Converse, S. L., Court, C., Foster, M., Lao, R., Oakley, J. D., & Smith, J. (1973). *Automatic Novel Writing: A Status Report* (Tech report 186). University of Wisconsin Computer Science Dept.

3 For some computer-generated story extracts in this book, we have converted uppercase text to lowercase and added capital letters to names and at the start of sentences to make the text more readable. Also, where a story is output by the computer one sentence to a line, in some cases we have let the text run on. Aside from this, the story is shown as output by the computer program. For stories generated by the GPT programs, the punctuation and layout are shown exactly as output by the program.

4 Wilson, G. (1971). The science fiction horror movie pocket computer. *National Lampoon*, November. Published here with permission of the current owners of the *National Lampoon* brand.

5 Propp, V. (1968). *Morphology of the Folktale*. University of Texas Press.

6 A story outline isn't quite the same as a plot. A plot is the sequence of significant events in a story, where one event causes or leads to another. A story outline shows the overall structure of a story but not necessarily how one event leads to another.

7 Smith, T. C., & Witten, I. H. (1991). *A Planning Mechanism for Generating Story Text* (Research Report 91/431/15). Department of Computer Science, University of Calgary. https://prism.ucalgary.ca/bitstream/handle/1880/46185/1991-431-15.pdf.

8 Meehan, J. R. (1976). *The Metanovel: Writing Stories by Computer*. Unpublished PhD Thesis, Yale University.

9 Get your document's readability and level statistics. Microsoft Support. https://bit.ly/2UkKXXz.

10 Turner, T. R. (1994). *The Creative Process: A Computer Model of Storytelling and Creativity*. Lawrence Erlbaum Associates.

11 Casebourne, I. (1996). The Grandmother program: A hybrid system for automated story generation. In *Proceedings of the Second International Symposium of Creativity and Cognition*, pp. 146–155. Loughborough University.

12 Melpomene & Uniwersytet Jagielloński (1980). *Bagabone, Hem 'I Die Now*. Vantage Press.

13 Racter (1984). *The Policeman's Beard Is Half Constructed*. Warner Books.

14 Dewdney, A. K. (1985). Artificial insanity: When a schizophrenic program meets a computerized analyst. Computer recreations. *Scientific American*, January. Lewis, P. H. (1985). Peripherals; A new brand of lunacy for sale. *The New York Times*, May 14.

15 French, S. (1993). *Just This Once*. Carol Publishing Group.

16 Radford, A., Wu, J., Child, R., Luan, D., Amodei, D., & Sutskever, I. (2019). Language models are unsupervised multitask learners. *OpenAI Blog*, 1(8), 9.

17 The first person voice in this story opening is distinctly different from *Nineteen Eighty-Four*, which continues "Winston Smith, his chin nuzzled into his breast in an effort to escape the vile wind, slipped quickly through the glass doors of Victory Mansions".

18 Hao, K. (2020). OpenAI is giving Microsoft exclusive access to its GPT-3 language model. *MIT Technology Review*, September 23.

19 www.machinewrites.com.

20 www.copy.ai.

21 Giving characters life with GPT3, https://fable-studio.com/behind-the-scenes/ai-generation. Create and distribute the story of your AI Virtual Being, https://fable-studio.com/wizard.

Chapter 2 Human story machines

1 For more about neuroscience and storytelling, see Armstrong, P. B. (2020). *Stories and the Brain: The Neuroscience of Narrative*. Johns Hopkins University Press. A related article is Armstrong, P. B. (2019). Neuroscience, narrative, and narratology. *Poetics Today*, 40(3), 395–428.

2 https://eagleman.com/updates/brain-time/. Originally published as: Eagleman, D. M. (2009). Brain Time. In M. Brockman (ed.), *What's Next? Dispatches on the Future of Science*. Vintage.

3 Fazio, P., Cantagallo, A., Craighero, L., D'Ausilio, A., Roy, A. C., Pozzo, T., . . . Fadiga, L. (2009). Encoding of human action in Broca's area. *Brain*, 132(7), 1980–1988.

4 The dialogue was originally published in Sharples, M. (1999). *How We Write: Writing as Creative Design*. Routledge.

5 Mar, R. A., Li, J., Nguyen, A. T., & Ta, C. P. (2021). Memory and comprehension of narrative versus expository texts: A meta-analysis. *Psychonomic Bulletin & Review*, 1–18.

6 Kipling, R. (2019). *In Black and White: A Short Story Collection*. Miniature Masterpiece.

7 Schank, R. C., & Abelson, R. P. (1977). *Scripts, Plans, Goals and Understanding: An Inquiry into Human Knowledge Structures*. Lawrence Erlbaum Associates.

8 The MINSTREL program mentioned in Chapter 1 incorporates Schank's case-based reasoning. James Meehan, developer of the TALE-SPIN program, was a student of Schank.

9 This section is based on Ferretti, F., Adornetti, I., Chiera, A., Nicchiarelli, S., Magni, R., Valeri, G., & Marini, A. (2017). Mental time travel and language evolution: A narrative account of the origins of human communication. *Language Sciences*, 63, 105–118.

10 Russon, A. E., & Andrews, K. (2011). Pantomime in great apes: Evidence and implications. *Communicative & Integrative Biology*, 4(3), 315–317.

11 Smith, D., Schlaepfer, P., Major, K., Dyble, M., Page, A. E., Thompson, J., . . . Migliano, A. B. (2017). Cooperation and the evolution of hunter-gatherer storytelling. *Nature Communications*, 8(1), 1–9.

12 For a summary, see the entry in *Encyclopedia Britannica*: www.britannica.com/topic/Epic-of-Gilgamesh.

13 www.britishmuseum.org/collection/object/W_K-3375.

14 Reimann, N. (2021). Feds take ownership of smuggled ancient "epic of Gilgamesh" tablet owned by hobby lobby. *Forbes*, July 27. www.forbes.com/sites/nicholasreimann/2021/07/27/feds-take-ownership-of-smuggled-ancient-epic-of-gilgamesh-tablet-owned-by-hobby-lobby/.

15 This example is taken verbatim from Sharples, 1999. The essay by Umberto Eco is: Eco, U. (1982). The narrative structure in Fleming. In B. Waites, T. Bennett, & G. Martin (eds.), *Popular Culture: Past and Present*. Croom Helm, pp. 245–262.

16 Johnson, E. (2016). SpaceX CEO Elon Musk has done the "real" Iron Man several favors. *Vox*, October 12. www.vox.com/2016/10/12/13259344/elon-musk-iron-man-jon-favreau-tony-stark-spacex-recode-podcast.

17 Sister Furong: https://en.wikipedia.org/wiki/Sister_Furong; Emma Chamberlain: https://en.wikipedia.org/wiki/Emma_Chamberlain.

18 Virgil, *Aenis*, III, 560–575. Dryden translation, 1806.

19 Swift, J. (1726, 2010). *Gulliver's Travels*. Penguin Classics. In case you are wondering, the second of the bizarre and pointless experiments has become a reality. See Gabbatis, J. (2018). Human waste used to make "Marmite-like" food for astronauts. *The Independent*, January 26. www.independent.co.uk/news/science/astronauts-food-human-waste-marmite-iss-international-space-station-nasa-a8179451.html.

20 Scott, W. (1825). *Tales of the Crusaders, by the Author of "Waverley, Quentin Durward," &c.* Constable. Quoted in Robertson, M. (1988). Narrative logic, folktales and machines. *Orbis Litterarum*, 43, 1–19.

21 Dahl, R. (1953). The great automatic grammatizator. In R. Dahl (ed.), *Someone Like You*. Alfred A. Knopf.

22 www.sf-encyclopedia.com/entry/wordmills.

23 Burroughs, W. (1959). *Naked Lunch*. Olympia Press, p. 221.

24 Lecture delivered in Turin and other Italian cities, November 1967. Published in Calvino, I. (1997). *The Literature Machine*. Vintage, pp. 15–16.

Chapter 3 Artificial versifying

1 Two articles telling the story of the Egyptian Hall are: Bacon, G. (1902). The story of the Egyptian Hall. *The English Illustrated Magazine*, 231, 298–308. Abrahams, A. (1906). The Egyptian Hall, piccadilly, 1813–1873. *The Antiquary*, 2(2), 61–64.

2 One shilling in current currency is about £4 or US $5. There are many short articles describing the Eureka machine. One of the clearest and most comprehensive is Blandford, D. W. (1963). The Eureka. *Greece & Rome*, 10(1), 71–78. The Alfred Gillett Trust publishes a web page with links to an archivist's description of Eureka and a video of the restored machine.

3 Peter, J. (1677). *Artificial Versifying, or the Schoolboys Recreation*. John Sims.

4 The rhythm, or metre, of Latin language is based on short and long intonation (unlike English, where the rhythm comes from stressing certain syllables). Here's a line of genuine Latin poetry showing the rhythm of long (e.g., ī) and short (e.g., ă) vowels: Trīstĭă rōbūstīs lūctāntūr fūnĕră plāūstrīs. Horace, *Ep.* ii. 2.74, cited in Blandford, D. (1963). The Eureka. *Greece and Rome*, 10(1), 71–78.

5 In the terms used to describe poetic metre, the sequence for Artificial Versifying is: dactyl trochee iamb molossus dactyl trochee.

6 For a brief overview of the teaching of Latin verse in English schools, see Adams, M. (2017). Latin verse composition in English schools 1500–1900. *The Classics Library*. Blog page. www.theclassicslibrary.com/latin-verse-composition-in-english-schools-1500-1900/.

7 For a short biography of John Clark, see Woolrich, A. P. (2011, expanded 2020). *John Clark 1785–1853*. Bridgwater Scientists, Bridgwater Heritage Group. www.bridgwaterscientists.org.uk/clarkJ/.

8 Cited in Virahsawmy, K. (n.d.). *John Clark (1785–1853)*. Alfred Gillett Trust. https://poetrybynumbers.exeter.ac.uk/history/johnclark/.

9 Description of the Latin Verse Machine from the Alfred Gillett Trust. https://nanopdf.com/download/lvm-alfred-gillett-trust_pdf.

10 The illustration isn't drawn accurately and to scale. The spikes vary in length from 9 inches to less than half an inch. Each rod is 24 inches long, with only the middle third of its length marked with letters. The rods all descend together until each one is brought to rest on its spike. Each drum has up between 15 and 20 lines of spikes and each line has up to 12 spikes to make up the letters of its Latin word.

11 There was also intense argument about translating Greek and Latin hexameter verse into English. The Greek and Latin languages create poetic rhythm by varying long and short syllables. English does this by putting emphasis on parts of a word. Some poets, such as Henry Wadsworth Longfellow, attempted

to mimic classical rhythms in English poetry. Others, such as Edgar Allan Poe, claimed this was a futile exercise.

12 See, for example, Bauer, S. W. (2009). *What is Classical Education*. Blog post on the Well-Trained Mind website. https://welltrainedmind.com/a/classical-education/?v=79cba1185463. According to the article, classical education is a three-part process of training the mind (the *trivium*). The early years are spent in absorbing facts and laying the foundations of study. In middle school, students think through arguments. In high school, they learn to express themselves.

13 Clark, J. (1848). *The General History and Description of a Machine for Composing Hexameter Latin Verses*. Frederick Wood. Quoted in Hall, J. D. (2007). Popular prosody: Spectacle and the politics of Victorian versification. *Nineteenth-Century Literature*, 62(2), 222–249.

14 Clark, J. (1845). Letter to *The Athenaeum*, July 12, pp. 669–670.

15 For an intriguing discussion of the kaleidoscope as a machine for exploring creativity, see Summers-Stay, D. (2011). *Machinamenta*. Machinamenta publishing.

16 Poetry by Numbers was a joint project of the University of Exeter and the Alfred Gillett Trust. Its website is at http://poetrybynumbers.exeter.ac.uk/. The website for the Alfred Gillett Trust is https://alfredgilletttrust.org/.

17 Jarry, A. (1929). *Gestes et opinions du Docteur Faustroll pataphysicien: roman néo-scientifique, suivi de spéculations*. E. Fasquelle. Published in English as Jarry, A. (1996). *Exploits and Opinions of Dr Faustroll, Pataphysician*. Exact Change.

18 For an introduction to the Oulipo group and its productions, see Motte, W. F. (ed.). (1986, 1998). *Oulipo: A Primer of Potential Literature*. Dalkey Archive Press. The book is https://monoskop.org/images/a/a4/Motte_Warren_F_ed_Oulipo_A_Primer_of_Potential_Literature.pdf.

19 A valuable blog post from 2017 profiles the women of Oulipo. According to the article, during the 57 years since its founding, Oulipo inducted only five women into its ranks. Coolidge, S. (2017). Who are the women of Oulipo? *Blog Post*, April 12. Centre for the Art of Translation. www.catranslation.org/blog-post/who-are-the-women-of-oulipo/.

20 Perec, G. (1969). *La Disparition*. Gallimard. Translated into English as Perec, G. (G. Adair tr.) (2008) *A Void*. Vintage Classics.

21 A printed version of the book was published as: Queneau, R. (1961). *Cent mille milliards de poèmes*. Gallimard. An interactive web-based version, in English and in French, is at www.bevrowe.info/Queneau/QueneauRandom_v4.html.

22 Tzara T. (1920). *Dada Manifesto on Feeble Love and Bitter Love*. A text read by Tristan Tzara at the Povolotzky Gallery, Paris, December 12.

23 The web-based Dada Poem Generator can be accessed at http://www1.lasalle.edu/~blum/c340wks/DadaPoem.htm.

24 Accessorise like Kate in red earrings by Blaiz. *Mail Online*, July 13, 2021. www. dailymail.co.uk/femail/article-9779523/Kate-Middleton-wears-65-bold-beaded-earrings-boutique-London-brand-Wembley.html.

25 Chaudhari, V. (2019). This is the odd writing technique used by David Bowie, Kurt Cobain, and Bob Dylan! *NYK Daily*, October 7. https://nykdaily. com/2019/10/this-is-the-odd-writing-technique-used-by-david-bowie-kurt-cobain-and-bob-dylan/.

26 The poem is reproduced in Bloomfield, C. (2017). *Homographic Translations: A Brief History & Attempts at Trilingual Sentences*. Outranspo website. www. outranspo.com/homographic-translations-a-brief-history-of-the-constraint-attempts-at-trilingual-sentences/.

27 The Institute no longer runs a website, but there is a Facebook site at www. facebook.com/londoninstituteofpataphysics/.

28 McCartney, L. (1992). *Linda McCartney's Sixties: Portrait of an Era*. Bullfinch Press, p. 153.

29 https://en.wikipedia.org/wiki/Manchester_Mark_1.

30 Trethowan, I. (1949). The mechanical brain. *The Times*, June 11, p. 4. Turing's comment about a sonnet was a riposte to Professor Jefferson who had delivered a lecture on 9 June 1949 to the Royal College of Surgeons in London (reported the next day in *The Times*) where he said that not until a machine could write a sonnet or a concerto because of thoughts and emotions felt and not by the chance fall of symbols could we agree that machine equals brain. Jefferson, G. (1949). The mind of mechanical man. *British Medical Journal*, 1(4616), pp. 1105–1110.

31 Strachey included the love letter generator and its algorithm as an example for an article he wrote in the literary magazine *Encounter*. Strachey, C. (1954). The 'thinking' machine. *Encounter*, October, pp. 25–31.

32 Sharples, M. (1984). *Cognition, Computers and Creative Writing*. PhD thesis, Department of Artificial Intelligence, University of Edinburgh. A revised version of the thesis, with an additional chapter, was published as a book: Sharples, M. (1985). *Cognition, Computers and Creative Writing*. Ellis Horwood.

33 *My Poetry generator passed the Turing Test*. Blog posting by Zachary Scholl, April 15, 2015. https://rpiai.com/other/poetry/.

34 Gnoetry is a bunch of people who write poetry using computer programs. For more detail, see https://gnoetrydaily.wordpress.com/about/.

35 Hartman, C. O. (1995). *Sentences*. Sun & Moon Books. Hartman started with a 19th-century grammar book, ran it through the TRAVESTY computer program for generating literary parodies, then ran the result through his own program DIASTEXT, based on the "diastic" writings of poet Jackson Mac Low. He describes the result as wonderfully eccentric poetry

that resembles something between Gertrude Stein and Surrealist automatic writing.

36 Some poetry generation sites are: www.poem-generator.org.uk/quick/, www. proflowers.com/blog/love-poetry-generator, www.poemofquotes.com/tools/poetry-generator/.

37 https://nickm.com/, www.alexsaum.com/, https://leonardoflores.net/.

38 "I got an Alligator for a Pet", a novel by @pentametron. https://pentametron.com/alligator.pdf.

39 Our thanks go to our Editor at Routledge, Bruce Roberts, for this phrase. Pentametron is an automated version of "found poetry", which borrows words or lines from other sources and forms them into all or part of a poem, like a literary collage. Bern Porter was a notable author of found poetry. A scientist who contributed to innovations such as the cathode ray tube, he also produced books of poetry compiled from product labels, everyday sayings, advertising slogans and much else. www.moma.org/calendar/exhibitions/1054.

Chapter 4 Automatic novel writers

1 During this period there were other lesser-known projects to build computer programs that generated stories, including Little Grey Rabbit (www.in-vacua.com/cgi-bin/rabbit_all.pl) and Grimes' fairy tale generator. www.researchgate.net/profile/James_Ryan32/publication/319301897_Grimes'_Fairy_Tales_A_1960s_Story_Generator/links/59a72c214585156873cfce3d/Grimes-Fairy-Tales-A-1960s-Story-Generator.pdf.

2 Maggie Davis, writer of women's fiction, quoted in Boudreau, J. (1993). A romance novel with byte: Author teams ups with computer to write book in steamy style of Jacqueline Susann. *Los Angeles Times*, August 11. www.latimes.com/archives/la-xpm-1993-08-11-vw-22645-story.html.

3 Klein's page at the University of Wisconsin is still http://pages.cs.wisc.edu/~sklein/sklein.html.

4 The extract is in an appendix to Klein, S. et al. (1973). *Automatic Novel Writing: A Status Report* (Technical Report #186). Computer Sciences Department, The University of Wisconsin. The University of Wisconsin.

5 The most notable critic was James Meehan in his PhD thesis, Meehan, J. (1976). *The Metanovel: Writing Stories by Computer*. PhD thesis, Yale University. James Ryan gives a fair and thorough account of "Klein's misunderstood system" in his PhD dissertation, Ryan, J. (2018). *Curating Simulated Storyworlds*. PhD thesis, University of California. For a forensic examination of Klein's murder mystery generator, see Ryan, M.-L. (1987). The heuristics of automatic story generation. *Poetics*, 16(6), 505–534.

6 The dialogue between Ed Kahn and Sheldon Klein is in Kahn, E., & Klein, S. (1974). Automatic novel writing – an exchange. *SIGART Newsletter*, April, pp. 3–5. Cited in Ryan (2018), op. cit.

7 Klein, S., Ross, D. A., Manasse, M. S., Danos, J., Bickford, M. S., Jensen, K. I., . . . Blanks, W. T. (1982). Propositional & analogical generation of coordinated verbal, visual & musical texts. *ACM SIGART Bulletin*, 79, 104. In an interview with *Byte* magazine, Klein states that "the music is superb but the action is quite dull", consisting of geometric shapes moving slowly around the screen. McKean, K. (1982). Computers, fiction, and poetry. *Byte*, July 7.

8 Klein, S. (2002). The analogical foundations of creativity in language, culture & the arts: The upper paleolithic to 2100 CE. *Advances in Consciousness Research*, 35, 347–372.

9 Racter (1984). *The Policeman's Beard Is Half Constructed*. Warner Books. The full text of the book is reproduced at www.ubu.com/concept/racter.html and a digitized copy of the pages can be downloaded from http://f17webadvanced. teachinginter.net/contents/pdfs/RACTER_Policemans-Beard.pdf.

10 A well-researched, though highly critical, account of the book and later commercial version of Racter is Henrickson, L. (2018). The policeman's beard is algorithmically constructed. *3:AM Magazine*, July 16. www.3ammagazine. com/3am/the-policemans-beard-is-algorithmically-constructed/.

11 Go to www.myabandonware.com/game/racter-4m and click on "Play in your browser" to hold a conversation with Racter. The dialogue in this book was from an interaction with this web version of Racter.

12 www.madlibs.com.

13 Ryan (2018), op. cit. The later paper by Henrickson (op. cit.) examines how the book was produced and by whom.

14 https://visualmelt.com/Racter.

15 https://web.archive.org/web/20120716194030/www.robotwisdom.com/ai/ racterfaq.html. This article from the 1993 issue of *The Journal of Computer Game Design* gives details of the computer code for INRAC.

16 Henrickson (2018), op. cit.

17 Melpomene & Uniwersytet Jagielloński (1980). *Bagabone, Hem 'I Die Now*. Vantage Press.

18 A photographic copy of the entire book is at https://archive.org/details/ xfoml0002/mode/2up.

19 Schultz, B. (1980). Publisher claims computer wrote novel. *Computerworld*, August 25, p. 23. https://books.google.co.uk/books?id=ZD0x4O_ruUAC&pg= PA23&redir_esc=y#v=onepage&q&f=false.

20 Michie, D., & Johnston, R. (1984). *The Creative Computer: Machine Intelligence and Human Knowledge*. Penguin Books Ltd.

21 Photographic scan of *Bagabone, Hem 'I Die Now*: https://archive.org/details/ xfoml0002.

22 French, S. (1993). *Just This Once*. Carol Publishing Group.

23 Podolsky, J. D. (1993). Byte by byte. *People.com*, October 11. https://people. com/archive/byte-by-byte-vol-40-no-15/.

24 Lohr, S. (1993). Potboiler springs from computer's loins. *New York Times*, July 2. www.nytimes.com/1993/07/02/us/media-business-encountering-digital-age-occasional-look-computers-everday-life.html.

25 Knight-Ridder Newspapers (1991). Computer turns page on rules of writing fiction. *Chicago Tribune*, March 18. www.chicagotribune.com/news/ct-xpm-1991-03-18-9101240900-story.html.

26 Publishers Weekly (1993). Just this once: A novel written by a computer programmed to think like the world's bestselling author. *Publishers Weekly*, May 3. www.publishersweekly.com/978-1-55972-173-8.

27 Bordreau, J. (1993). A romance novel with byte: Author teams ups with computer to write book in steamy style of Jacqueline Susann. *Los Angeles Times*, August 11. www.latimes.com/archives/la-xpm-1993-08-11-vw-22645-story. html.

28 An out-of-date list of computer-generated books is at https://nickm.com/ post/2016/07/computer-generated-books/.

29 Cope describes his program in Cope, D. (2020). *The Computer-Generated Novel*. Epoc Books.

30 The original impetus for NatNoGenMo came from a Tweet by Darius Kazemi: "Hey, who wants to join me in NaNoGenMo: spend the month writing code that generates a 50k word novel, share the novel & the code at the end". The rules for entry are at https://nanogenmo.github.io/. This also lists the completed works and gives links to their code.

31 *The Annals of the Parrigues* can be downloaded for a voluntary donation as a PDF at https://inthewalls.itch.io/parrigues.

32 Montfort, N. (2018). *Hard West Turn*. Bad Quarto. The book web page gives a link to the computer code that generated it: https://badquar.to/publications/ hard_west_turn.html. The website for the Using Electricity book series is at http://counterpathpress.org/using-electricity.

Chapter 5 The shape of a story

1 Klein, S., Aeschlimann, J. F., Balsiger, D. F., Converse, S. L., Foster, M., Lao, R., . . . Smith, J. (1973). *Automatic Novel Writing: A Status Report* (Technical report #186). University of Wisconsin-Madison Department of Computer Sciences.

2 The scholar Serena Vitale recorded a series of interviews with Victor Shklovsky in 1978. In these he reminisced about his life and works, including his

entanglements in St Petersburg with Futurists and Formalists. The interviews are published in Vitale, S. (2012). *Shklovsky: Witness to an Era* (tr. J. Richards). Dalkey Archive Press. For a brief biography of Shklovsky, see Ehrenreich, B. (2013). Making strange: On Victor Shklovsky. *The Nation*, February 5. www. thenation.com/article/archive/making-strange-victor-shklovsky/.

3 It is also written as "Opojaz". We use the spelling in Vitale (2012). For more on Opoyaz and Russian Formalism, see Mambrol, N. (2020). Russian formalism. *Literary Theory and Criticism*, October 19. https://literariness.org/2020/10/19/russian-formalism/.

4 "Literary works, according to this model, resemble machines: they are the result of an intentional human activity in which a specific skill transforms raw material into a complex mechanism suitable for a particular purpose", Steiner, P. (1995). Russian formalism. In R. Selden (ed.), *The Cambridge History of Literary Criticism, Volume 8: From Formalism to Poststructuralism*. Cambridge University Press.

5 Poet Elizaveta Grigorevna Polonskaya attended Shklovsky's lectures and was the sole female member of the Serapion Brotherhood, a group of nonconformist writers loosely associated with the Formalists.

6 Good writing can be deliberately unsettling. Stories written by computer have the potential to make objects unfamiliar and literary forms difficult by creating language and plots that are plausible in context but unlikely to be crafted by a human writer.

7 Shklovsky, V. (1990). *Theory of Prose* (tr. B. Sher). Dalkey Archive Press.

8 For an overview of Propp's life and work, see Levin, I. (1967). Vladimir Propp: An evaluation on his seventieth birthday. *Journal of the Folklore Institute*, 4(1), 32–49.

9 Propp, V. (1968). *Morphology of the Folktale* (tr. L. Scott). University of Indiana Press.

10 See www.joelhunterphd.com/folktale-structure-key-success-harry-potter-series/, which analyzes each of the Harry Potter books in terms of Propp's formulas.

11 Lévi-Strauss, C. (1955). The structural study of myth. *The Journal of American Folklore*, 68(270), 428–444.

12 Alan Dundes gives an excellent account in Dundes, A. (1997). Binary opposition in myth: The Propp/Lévi-Strauss debate in retrospect. *Western Folklore*, 56(1), 39–50. According to Dundes, both Propp and Lévi-Strauss attempted to analyze the structure of stories. Whereas Propp studied the order of events as presented in the narrative, Lévi-Strauss looked for contrasts between the underlying themes. What particularly annoyed Propp was that Lévi-Strauss regarded fairy stories as unworthy of study and the linear form of narrative as obvious and superficial. Propp was also insulted by the suggestion from Lévi-Strauss

that he (Propp) wasn't skilled enough to understand myths. Propp retorted that Lévi-Strauss had carried out his analyses in complete disregard to the structure of the narratives. Lévi-Strauss had the last word in the debate with a postscript to Propp's rebuttal where he claimed he had merely been offering "a homage" to Propp's pioneering work.

13 Propp (1968), op. cit., p. 111.

14 The description in this chapter of the work of Joseph E. Grimes is largely based on the work of James Ryan in uncovering and promoting early contributions to story generation. Ryan carried out a series of interviews with Grimes and commissioned a translation from Spanish of his written account of his system. See Ryan, J. (2017). Grimes' fairy tales: A 1960s story generator. In *Proceedings of International Conference on Interactive Digital Storytelling*. Springer, pp. 89–103. A longer account is in Ryan's PhD thesis: Ryan, J. (2018). *Curating Simulated Storyworlds*. PhD dissertation, University of California.

15 Klein, S., Aeschlimann, J. F., . . . Salsieder, D. F. (1974). *Modelling Propp and Lévi-Strauss in a Meta-Symbolic Simulation System* (Technical Report #226). Computer Sciences Department, The University of Wisconsin.

16 Lakoff, G. P. (1972). Structural complexity in fairy tales. *The Study of Man*, 1, 128–150. In a footnote, Lakoff writes: "This paper was written in 1964 while my remote ancestor, George P. Lakoff was a graduate student at Indiana University."

17 Pemberton, L. (1989). A modular approach to story generation. In *Proceedings of Fourth Conference of the European Chapter of the Association for Computational Linguistics*. Manchester, pp. 217–224.

Chapter 6 The program that swallowed the internet

1 The Guardian (2019). New AI fake text generator may be too dangerous to release, say creators. *The Guardian*, February 14. www.theguardian.com/technology/2019/feb/14/elon-musk-backed-ai-writes-convincing-news-fiction.

2 The human brain has about 80 billion neurons with 100 trillion connections. The largest neural networks have about 16 million neurons, though that number is increasing rapidly. Besides neurons, there are other elements, including interconnections between neurons and connections to other body systems, that give brains their cognitive abilities.

3 The example is in Foster, D. (2019). *Generative Deep Learning: Teaching Machines to Paint, Write, Compose and Play*. O'Reilly Media, Inc.

4 Goodfellow, I., Pouget-Abadie, J., Mirza, M., Xu, B., Warde-Farley, D., Ozair, S., . . . Bengio, Y. (2020). Generative adversarial networks. *Communications of the ACM*, 63(11), 139–144.

5 A blog review of a neural network research paper in June 2017 by the computational linguist Yoav Goldberg starts "for fucks sake DL people, leave language alone and stop saying you solve it". Goldberg, Y. (2017). An adversarial review of "adversarial generation of natural language". *Blog Post*, June 9. https://medium.com/@yoav.goldberg/an-adversarial-review-of-adversarial-generation-of-natural-language-409ac3378bd7.

6 Vaswani, A., Shazeer, N., Parmar, N., Uszkoreit, J., Jones, L., Gomez, A. N., . . . Polosukhin, I. (2017). Attention is all you need. In *Advances in Neural Information Processing Systems*, pp. 5998–6008. This wasn't the first paper to propose an attention mechanism, but it showed how the mechanism alone can generate well-formed text. The mechanism was proposed in Bahdanau, D., Cho, K., & Bengio, B. (2015). Neural machine translation by jointly learning to align and translate. Paper presented at 3rd International Conference on Learning Representations, ICLR. https://arxiv.org/abs/1409.0473.

7 Whigham, N. (2019). This AI is so good at writing, its creators won't release it. *New York Post*, February 19. https://nypost.com/2019/02/19/this-ai-is-so-good-at-writing-its-creators-wont-release-it/.

8 Brown, T. B., Mann, B., Ryder, N., Subbiah, M., Kaplan, J., Dhariwal, P., . . . Amodei, D. (2020). Language models are few-shot learners. *arXiv:2005.14165*. https://arxiv.org/pdf/2005.14165.pdf.

9 Li, C. (2020). *OpenAI's GPT-3 Language Model: A Technical Overview*. Lambda Labs. https://lambdalabs.com/blog/demystifying-gpt-3/.

10 Marche, S. (2021). The computers are getting better at writing. *The New Yorker*, April 30. www.newyorker.com/culture/cultural-comment/the-computers-are-getting-better-at-writing.

11 OpenAI (2020). *OpenAI API*. Blog posting from OpenAI. https://openai.com/blog/openai-api/.

12 Montavon, G., Samek, W., & Müller, K. R. (2018). Methods for interpreting and understanding deep neural networks. *Digital Signal Processing*, 73, 1–15.

13 Other language generators include BERT (developed at Google), Turing NLG (from Microsoft) and Megatron (developed by Nvidia). They come from large corporations rather than research labs because of the huge cost in computer time to train these systems, though they all build on many years of research from academic researchers. Never outdone in artificial intelligence, China has developed an AI language model with 1.57 trillion interconnections. WuDao 2.0, developed at the Beijing Academy of Artificial Intelligence can combine text, audio and pictures, for example, to generate pictures from written descriptions and to power virtual pop idols. www.engadget.com/chinas-gigantic-multi-modal-ai-is-no-one-trick-pony-211414388.html.

14 Mori, M. (1970, trans. 2012). The Uncanny Valley, tr. Karl F. MacDorman & Norri Kageki. *IEEE Spectrum*, June 12. https://spectrum.ieee.org/automaton/robotics/humanoids/the-uncanny-valley.

15 When the computer as storyteller is taken from the realms of fantasy and put into service as a newsreader or weather forecaster, then we apply a different criterion. We expect a news item to be accurate rather than entertaining.

Chapter 7 Storyworlds

1 Owen, W., & Smyser, J. (1974). *The Prose Works of William Wordsworth* (Vol. 1). Clarendon Press, p. 148.

2 The full text of The Prelude is at https://archive.org/stream/preludeorgrowtho00wordiala/preludeorgrowtho00wordiala_djvu.txt.

3 The US company Boston Dynamics builds humanoid robots that can run, climb and dance, as well as walk over rugged terrain. www.bostondynamics.com/.

4 For a detailed account of Colossal Cave Adventure and the Colossal Cave that inspired it, see Jerz, D. G. (2007). Somewhere nearby is Colossal Cave: Examining Will Crowther's original "Adventure" in code and in Kentucky. *Digital Humanities Quarterly*, 1(2), 2. http://jerz.setonhill.edu/resources/preprint/SNiCC.pdf.

5 A free online version of the game is available at https://grack.com/demos/adventure/.

6 Colossal Cave Adventure recognizes a limited set of commands such as "go south", "enter building", "take lamp". Later text-based games such as Zork and The Dreamhold recognize complete sentences such as "Put the lamp on the table". The storyworld for Adventure was mapped out in advance by the designers. Some modern adventure games such as AI Dungeon can generate new settings and storylines. https://en.wikipedia.org/wiki/AI_Dungeon.

7 See www.sierrahelp.com/Walkthroughs/AdventureWalkthrough.html for a Colossal Cave Adventure walkthrough.

8 www.statista.com/statistics/246888/value-of-the-global-video-game-market/.

9 A book based on Mike's thesis is Sharples, M. (1985). *Cognition, Computers and Creative Writing*. Ellis Horwood.

10 The names of the children have been changed.

11 This is a fascinating account of how video games are designed, from the perspective of storytelling: Skolnick, E. (2014). *Video Game Storytelling: What Every Developer Needs to Know about Narrative Techniques*. Watson-Guptill Publications.

12 For an overview of LIGHT, see https://parl.ai/projects/light/?fbclid=IwAR1VViik0woKB1hxPGlHvVYdJ43SEZqOpRYm_f2TwqQwKTFvX5Aukc-xANo.

An academic paper on the project is Urbanek, J., Fan, A., Karamcheti, S., Jain, S., Humeau, S., Dinan, E., . . . Weston, J. (2019). Learning to speak and act in a fantasy text adventure game. *arXiv preprint* https://arxiv.org/abs/1903.03094.

13 Schank, R. (1972). Conceptual dependency: A theory of natural language understanding. *Cognitive Psychology*, 3, 552–631.

14 Grand Text Auto is a blog about computer narrative, games, poetry and art. It has an article on the background of TALE-SPIN, including an interview with James Meehan. Wardrip-Fruin, N. (2006). The story of Meehan's TALE-SPIN. *Grand Text Auto*, September 13. https://grandtextauto.soe.ucsc.edu/2006/09/13/the-story-of-meehans-TALE-SPIN/. For an overview of the TALE-SPIN program, see Meehan, J. R. (1977). TALE-SPIN, an interactive program that writes stories. In *Proceedings of 5th International Joint Conference on Artificial Intelligence*, August, pp. 91–98. www.ijcai.org/Proceedings/77-1/Papers/013.pdf.

15 Labov and Waltzky examined personal stories that one friend tells to another, concluding that people will be more likely to pay attention to stories that are both reportable and credible. Labov, W., & Waletzky, J. (1967). Narrative analysis: Oral versions of personal experience. In J. Helm (ed.), *Essays on the Verbal and Visual Arts*. University of Washington Press, pp. 12–44.

16 Meehan did write a rudimentary program to automatically translate the Schank and Abelson Conceptual Dependency notation into English. The story starting "George was very thirsty" is an example of its output.

17 Ryan, J. O., Summerville, A., Mateas, M., & WardripFruin, N. (2015). Toward characters who observe, tell, misremember, and lie. In *Proceedings of the Workshop on Experimental AI in Games*. https://eis.ucsc.edu/papers/ryanEtAl_TowardCharactersWhoObserveTellMisrememberLie.pdf.

18 Interview with Chinua Achebe by Jerome Brooks in *The Paris Review*, The Art of Fiction, No. 139, Issue 133, Winter 1994. www.theparisreview.org/interviews/1720/the-art-of-fiction-no-139-chinua-achebe.

19 This project and others on curating stories from games is described in detail by James Ryan in his PhD thesis: Ryan, J. (2018). *Curating Simulated Storyworlds*. PhD dissertation, University of California Santa Cruz. https://escholarship.org/content/qt1340j5h2/qt1340j5h2.pdf.

20 The name Sheldon is Ryan's nod to the ubiquitous Sheldon Klein.

21 https://soundcloud.com/james-ryan-887346009/episode-2-the-good-stuff.

22 Montfort, N. (2011). Curveship's automatic narrative style. In *Proceedings of the 6th International Conference on Foundations of Digital Games*, June 28–July 1. Bordeaux, France, pp. 211–218. https://dspace.mit.edu/handle/1721.1/67645.

23 The website to download and play Dwarf Fortress is at www.bay12games.com/dwarves/.

24 Interview with Tarn Adams by Wes Fenlon of *PC Gamer*, including the dead cats incident: Fenlon, W. (2016). Dwarf Fortress' creator on how he's 42% towards simulating existence. *PC Gamer*, March 31. www.pcgamer.com/uk/dwarf-fortress-creator-on-how-hes-42-towards-simulating-existence/.

Chapter 8 Being creative

1 Morley, D. (2007). *The Cambridge Introduction to Creative Writing*. Cambridge University Press, p. 2.

2 https://alumni.media.mit.edu/~mueller/.

3 Mueller, E. T. (1990). *Daydreaming in Humans and Machines: A Computer Model of the Stream of Thought*. Ablex Publishing Corporation.

4 The Cog website is still www.ai.mit.edu/projects/humanoid-robotics-group/cog/cog.html.

5 Boden, M. A. (1994). What is creativity? In M. A. Boden (ed.), *Dimensions of Creativity*. The MIT Press, p. 79.

6 For a short account of how *West Side Story* was conceived see Catton, P. (2018). "West Side Story" was originally about Jews and Catholics. *History Blog*. www.history.com/news/west-side-story-was-originally-about-jews-and-catholics.

7 The anecdote about Propp is in Turner's book. See also https://heredragonsabound.blogspot.com/p/about-scott-turner.html.

8 Turner, S. (1994). *The Creative Process: A Computer Model of Storytelling and Creativity*. Lawrence Erlbaum Associates.

9 Ibid., p. 10.

10 We first gave this example in Pérez y Pérez, R., & Sharples, M. (2004). Three computer-based models of storytelling: Brutus, Minstrel and Mexica. *Knowledge-Based Systems*, 17(1), 15–29.

11 The ConceptNet website (https://conceptnet.io/) offers an admirably simple demonstration of its powers. You type in a word or phrase (from over 30 languages), click Search, and it shows how the concept for that word relates to other concepts (for example, for "needle", how and where a needle is used, properties of needles). Clicking on any of these (such as "sewing machine") brings up concepts linked to that word, and so on through the network of concepts.

12 For a discussion of proof by demonstration in relation to research methods for computing, see Holz, H. J., Applin, A., Haberman, B., Joyce, D., Purchase, H., & Reed, C. (2006). Research methods in computing: What are they, and how should we teach them? In *Working Group Reports on ITiCSE on Innovation and Technology in Computer Science Education*. ITiCSE'06 Conference, pp. 96–114. http://pooh.poly.asu.edu/Ser515/Schedule/docs/cs-research-methods.pdf.

13 The AlphaZero computer program developed by the DeepMind AI company learned to play chess by being given only the rules of the game, then playing millions of games against itself. After nine hours of self-training, it was able to beat the best previous chess program (Stockfish) without losing a game. A chess expert describes its play style as "alien". It sometimes wins by outrageous moves, such as sacrificing a queen and bishop. AlphaZero searches many fewer board states each game than a conventional chess program (40 thousand, compared with up to 70 million for Stockfish), but that's still very different from a human chess expert who doesn't search thousands of board positions each move, but instead recognizes patterns of pieces on the board and uses that pattern recognition to guide where to move. See Silver, D., Hubert, T., Schrittwieser, J., Antonoglou, I., Lai, M., Guez, A., . . . Hassabis, D. (2018). A general reinforcement learning algorithm that masters chess, shogi, and Go through self-play. *Science*, 362(6419), 1140–1144.

14 Turner (1994), op. cit., p. 282.

Chapter 9 Modelling the mind of a writer

1 For an article about AI applied to weather forecasting, see Hickey, H. (2020). A.I. model shows promise to generate faster, more accurate weather forecasts. *UW News,* University of Washington, December 15. www.washington.edu/news/2020/12/15/a-i-model-shows-promise-to-generate-faster-more-accurate-weather-forecasts/.

2 Other ways to describe how people write include stage models (prewrite, draft, revise, edit), structural models (of how characters, themes, plots and genres fit together), analytic models (to find patterns across stories), and social-constructivist theories of how writing is conditioned by media and society, see https://sun.iwu.edu/~writcent/writing_processes.htm.

3 *The Paris Review Interviews* is a collection of interviews with great writers – including Dorothy Parker, Truman Capote, Ernest Hemingway, T. S. Eliot, Saul Bellow, and Jorge Luis Borges – where they describe their craft in revealing detail. www.theparisreview.org/interviews.

4 King, S. (2000). *On Writing: A Memoir of the Craft*. Hodder & Stoughton Ltd.

5 There are many problems with this method (it's not easy – some would say it's impossible – to concurrently speak and write), but it did influence early cognitive models of writing.

6 Sharples, M. (1994). Computer support for the rhythms of writing. *Computers and Composition*, 11(3), 217–226.

7 One book we found helpful is Lawson, B. (2005). *How Designers Think: The Design Process Demystified* (fourth edition). Routledge. It is more about creative

problem-solving than visual design but it helped us to see writing as a design process.

8 For more detail, see Sharples, M. (1999). *How We Write: Writing as Creative Design*. Routledge. For a description of how MEXICA works, see Pérez y Pérez, R., & Sharples, M. (2001). MEXICA: A computer model of a cognitive account of creative writing. *Journal of Experimental & Theoretical Artificial Intelligence*, 13(2), 119–139. A book of 20 stories generated by MEXICA, in English and Spanish, is Pérez y Pérez, R. (2017). *MEXICA: 20 Years – 20 Stories*. Counterpath Press.

9 King (2000), op. cit., p. 196.

10 If you are stuck for inspiration, you could turn to a "what-if" program that churns out primary generators such as "What if mass production had been invented a hundred years later?", "What if today's most commonplace technology was mind control?", "What if you went to the hospital for a routine operation and woke up to discover that they'd performed the wrong surgery on you?". https://mycuprunsover.ca/writing-prompt-generator-kids/ and www.seventhsanctum.com/generate.php?Genname=whatif.

11 https://harrypotter.bloomsbury.com/uk/jk-rowling-biography.

12 The distinction between high focus and low focus thinking is from Gelernter, D. (1994). *The Muse in the Machine: Computers and Creative Thought*. Fourth Estate.

13 Freud, S. (1959). Creative writers and daydreaming. In J. Strachey (ed.), *Standard Edition of the Complete Psychological Works of Sigmund Freud* (Vol. 9). Hogarth Press, pp. 141–153.

14 King (2000), op. cit., p. 249.

15 www.britishcouncil.org/voices-magazine/seven-lessons-roald-dahl-how-be-productive.

16 Ihde, D. (1979). *Technics and Praxis*. Reidl, p. 43.

17 I (Rafael) have written versions of text for MEXICA in English and Spanish. The book of 20 MEXICA stories is, thus, a collaboration between MEXICA (generating the story outlines) and myself and colleague Nick Montfort (adding the text for each story element).

18 The term "docuverse" was coined by computer scientist and visionary Ted Nelson. He also invented the word "hypertext". His ideas inspired development of the World Wide Web.

Chapter 10 Build your own story generator

1 The approach and the headline grammar is based on an example in Sharples, M. (1999). *How We Write: Writing as Creative Design*. Routledge.

2 Headline in the *Sunday Sport* newspaper, August 21, 2011.

3 Headline generator at www.contentrow.com/tools/headline-generator.

4 Pring-Mill, R. (1990). The Lullian "art of finding truth": A medieval system of enquiry. *Catalan Review*, 4(1–2), 55–74.

5 They also included an analysis of elections and a fair voting system that is still in use. Faliszewski, P., Hemaspaandra, E., Hemaspaandra, L., & Rothe, J. (2009a). Llull and Copeland voting broadly resist bribery and control. *Journal of Artificial Intelligence Research*, 35, 275–341.

6 The diagram is based on Bonner, A. (2007). *The Art and Logic of Ramon Llull: A User's Guide*. Brill. The entire book is available online at https://uberty.org/wp-content/uploads/2015/12/Anthony_Bonner_The_art_and_logic_of_Ramon_Llull.pdf.

7 Fourth Figure. Ars brevis XVIII Century. Palma de Mallorca BP MS998. Digital version, Biblioteca Virtual del Patrimonio Bibliográfico. Spain. Ministerio de Educación, Cultura y Deporte.

8 Bonner (2007), op. cit., p. 151.

9 Fans of the His Dark Materials series by Philip Pullman may have noticed a similarity between Llull's disks and the alethiometer. In an interview with the magazine *Textualities*, Pullman claimed that the alethiometer came not directly from Llull but from his interest in the Renaissance. http://textualities.net/jennie-renton/philip-pullman-interview.

10 For example www.plot-generator.org.uk/ and https://blog.reedsy.com/plot-generator/.

Chapter 11 Capacity for empathy

1 We wrote Stories 1 and 3. The GPT-3 program generated Stories 2 and 4. We chose the titles for all four stories.

2 That is based on the current price for the Beta version of GPT-3. https://beta.openai.com/pricing.

3 "Write Better Marketing Copy, Effortlessly": https://writesonic.com/; "Get high quality content in under 60 seconds": www.articleforge.com/; "Generate Accurate, Relevant & Quality Content in 2 Minutes": https://ai-writer.com/.

4 Bakhtin, M. M. (1981). *The Dialogic Imagination: Four Essays* (ed. M. Holquist, tr. C. Emerson & M. Holquist). University of Texas Press.

5 Future of StoryTelling Spotlight Series (2019). Q&A with Pete Billington of Emmy Award – winning fable studio. *Medium*, October 2. https://link.medium.com/1XllfmpKehb.

6 Takahashi, D. (2020). Fable studio unveils two AI-based virtual beings who can talk to you. *VentureBeat*, December 18. https://venturebeat.com/2020/12/18/fable-studio-unveils-two-ai-based-virtual-beings-who-can-talk-to-you/.

7 Peiser, J. (2019). The rise of the robot reporter. *New York Times*, February 5. www.nytimes.com/2019/02/05/business/media/artificial-intelligence-journalism-robots.html.

8 Shewan, D. (2021). 10 of the most innovative chatbots on the web. *WordStream*, April 25. www.wordstream.com/blog/ws/2017/10/04/chatbots.

9 "Armchair travel experiences that let you explore the world from your living room". www.thrillist.com.au/travel/nation/virtual-trips-travel-tours/.

10 Lyons, K. (2020). A college student used GPT-3 to write fake blog posts and ended up at the top of hacker news. *The Verge*, August 16. www.theverge.com/2020/8/16/21371049/gpt3-hacker-news-ai-blog.

11 The Slant project combined MEXICA to generate plots with other components to model the storyworld, generate figurative language, and present the text using narrative techniques such as flashback. Montfort, N., Pérez y Pérez, R., Harrell, D. F., & Campana, A. (2013). Slant: A blackboard system to generate plot, figuration, and narrative discourse aspects of stories. In *Proceedings of the International Conference on Computational Creativity (ICCC) 2013*, Sydney, June 12–14, 2013, pp. 168–175.

12 Yao, L., Peng, N., Weischedel, R., Knight, K., Zhao, D., & Yan, R. (2019). Plan-and-write: Towards better automatic storytelling. In *Proceedings of the AAAI Conference on Artificial Intelligence* (Vol. 33, No. 1), July, pp. 7378–7385. The program has two modes for planning and writing. In dynamic mode, the program alternates between planning and writing. In static mode, it plans first, then writes.

13 Radio interview with author Kazuo Ishiguro on "The Today Programme", BBC Radio 4, March 1, 2021.

14 The International Space Station sends a continual live video feed from space: https://video.ibm.com/channel/iss-hdev-payload.

15 File Explorer: https://github.com/NaNoGenMo/2019/issues/25.

Further reading

Aarseth, E. J. (1997). *Cybertext: Perspectives on Ergodic Literature*. The Johns Hopkins University Press.

Adger, D. A. (2019). *Language Unlimited: The Science Behind Our Most Creative Power*. Oxford University Press.

Armstrong, P. B. (2020). *Stories and the Brain: The Neuroscience of Narrative*. Johns Hopkins University Press.

Boden, M. A. (2004). *The Creative Mind: Myths and Mechanisms*. Routledge.

Bringsjord, S., & Ferrucci, D. A. (2000). *Artificial Intelligence and Literary Creativity: Inside the Mind of BRUTUS, a Storytelling Machine*. Lawrence Erlbaum Associates.

Calvino, I. (1997). *The Literature Machine* (translated from the Italian by Patrick Creagh). Vintage Books.

Cope, D. (2020). *The Computer-Generated Novel*. Epoc Books.

du Sautoy, M. (2019). *The Creativity Code: How AI is Learning to Write, Paint and Think*. 4th Estate.

Foster, D. (2019). *Generative Deep Learning: Teaching Machines to Paint, Write, Compose and Play*. O'Reilly.

French, S. (1993). *Just This Once: A Novel Written by a Computer Programmed to Think Like the World's Bestselling Author (as told to Scott French)*. Carol Publishing Group.

King, S. (2000). *On Writing: A Memoir of the Craft*. Hodder & Stoughton.

Lee, K.-F., & Qiufan, C. (2021). *AI 2041: Ten visions for Our Future*. WH Allen.

Lodge, D. (1996). *The Practice of Writing*. Secker & Warburg.

Melpomene and Uniwersytet Jagielloński. (1980). *Bagabone, Hem 'I Die Now*. Vantage Press.

Miller, A. I. (2019). *The Artist in the Machine: The World of AI-Powered Creativity*. The MIT Press.

Montfort, N. (2015). *Twisty Little Passages: An Approach to Interactive Fiction*. The MIT Press.

Morley, D. (2007). *The Cambridge Introduction to Creative Writing*. Cambridge University Press.

Mueller, E. T. (1990). *Daydreaming in Humans and Machines: A Computer Model of the Stream of Thought*. Erik T. Mueller.

Murray, J. H. (2017). *Hamlet on the Holodeck: The Future of Narrative in Cyberspace* (updated edition). The MIT Press.

Pérez y Pérez, R. (ed.). (2015). *Creatividad Computacional*. Patria-UAM.

Pérez y Pérez, R. (2017). *MEXICA: 20 Years – 20 Stories*. Counterpath Press.

Propp, V. (1968). *Morphology of the Folktale* (second edition). University of Texas Press.

Racter. (1984). *The Policeman's Beard is Half Constructed*. Warner Books.

Sawyer, R. K. (2012). *Explaining Creativity: The Science of Human Innovation* (second edition). Oxford University Press.

Sharples, M. (1999). *How We Write: Writing as Creative Design*. Routledge.

Skolnick, E. (2014). *Video Game Storytelling: What Every Developer Needs to Know About Narrative Techniques*. Watson-Guptill Publications.

Summers Stay, D. (2011). *Machinamenta: The Thousand Year Quest to Build a Creative Machine*. Machinamenta Publishing.

Turner, Scott R. (1994). *The Creative Process: A Computer Model of Storytelling*. Lawrence Erlbaum Associates.

Veale, T. (2012). *Exploding the Creative Myth. The Computational Foundations of Linguistic Creativity*. Bloomsbury.

Veale, T. (2021). *Your Wit Is My Command: Building AIs With a Sense of Humor*. The MIT Press.

Veale, T., & Cardoso, F. A. (eds.). (2019). *Computational Creativity: The Philosophy and Engineering of Autonomously Creative Systems*. Springer.

Vitale, S. (2012). *Shklovsky: Witness to an Era* (translated by Jamie Richards). Dalkey Archive Press.

Wardrip-Fruin, N. (2009). *Expressive Processing: Digital Fictions, Computer Games, and Software Studies*. The MIT Press.

Weisberg, R. W. (1993). *Creativity: Beyond the Myth of Genius*. Freeman, 1993.

Index

Abelson, Robert 93
Adventure 90–91
Agta people 19
ALMA (Artificial Linguistic Machine Algorithm) 55
American humour magazine 3
animal communication 18
animators 146
Annals of the Parrigues, The 57
appealing, automatically 142
architects' models 124
Article Forge 144
artificial friend 149
artificial intelligence (AI): advertising copy 144; cognitive models 103; programmers 146; research 91
Artificial Linguistic Machine Algorithm (ALMA) 55
artificial versifying: computer poetry 41–43; creative constraint 36–39; Eureka clockwork *vs.* machine 30–32; hexameter mania 32–34; Latin verse machine 27–30; love letters from Manchester 39–40; Oulipo 34–36; Pentametron 43–44
Asimov, Isaac 25
Athenaeum, The 33
automated story writing 49
Automatic Grammatizator 24–25

automatic novel writers 3; approaches to story generation 56–57; *Bagabone, Hem 'I Die Now* 52–53; *Just This Once* 53–54; Klein's automatic novel writer 45–46; language rules and memory networks 48; murder mystery party 46–48; NaNoGenMo 54–56; *Policeman's Beard Is Half Constructed, The* 49–52

Babbage, Charles 30
Bagabone, Hem 'I Die Now 52–53
Bakhtin, Mikhail 145
Ballard, J. G. 25
Barthes, Roland 61–62
Battle of Algiers 22
Beatles, The 39
Beetle Boy 17
beliefs: and society 49; and utterances 145
Bezos, Jeff 22
Bhatnagar, Ranjit 44
Bitcoin 22
Bloomberg News 147
Boden, Margaret 106
Bowie, David 38
brand managers 22
Branson, Richard 22
Bruner, Jerome 82
Burroughs, William S. 25, 38

Calvino, Italo 25
Cambridge Introduction to Creative Writing, The 101
capitalism 37
capitalist society 38
Casebourne, Imogen 8
Cent Mille Milliards de Poèmes 35–36
Chamberlain, William 49
character, goal of 9
Chomsky, Noam 64–65
Clark, John 30, 33–36, 44, 149
Clarke, Arthur C. 25
clockwork *vs.* machine 30–32
Cobain, Kurt 38
coherence 116–117, 124
College of Pataphysics 35
Colossal Cave 91
Colossal Cave Adventure 84–87
combinatorial creativity 102
Communist Manifesto, The 70–71
completeness 23
computer: chess-playing programs 113; code 84; games 13, 96–97; gaming 40; -generated folk tales 63; -generated landmarks 147; -generated novel 54; -generated story 13; poetry 41–43; storyteller 99
Computerworld magazine 52
ConceptNet 112
conceptual creativity 106
Cope, David 55
courage 32
COVID-19 pandemic 15
creative cognition 142
creative constraint 36–39
creative writing 81, 150
Crowther, Will 84
culture and convention 22
cut-up method 38

Dahl, Roald 24, 118
Daily Mail newspaper 37
DAYDREAMER 103–105
daydreaming 103–105, 116
Daydreaming in Humans and Machines 103, 105
Deena's Lucky Penny 17
demonstrator systems 113

design imaginative worlds 149
digital docuverse 125
digital literature 40
digressions 19, 59
Disney 145–146
Disparition, La 35
dispatcher 60–61
dominated-dominant relationship 21
donor 61
Dousterswivel, Hermann 24
Dwarf Fortress 99–100
Dylan, Bob 38

Eco, Umberto 21–22
educational story books 17
electronic brains 39
electronic surveillance consultant 53
emotion/emotional 12–13, 44, 77, 83, 105, 148; bond 122; impact 116; intelligence 149; links and tensions 123; response 44, 77, 104
empathy, capacity for 150; language generation 143–145; life on internet, stories of 150–151; storytelling models 147–150; storyworlds 145–147
engagement and reflection 115, 117–119, 123–124
Epic of Gilgamesh 20
Etter, Thomas 49
Eureka machine 26, 32–36, 58, 71, 102
excursions 56
experiential creativity 103–105
Exploits and Opinions of Dr. Faustroll, Pataphysician 35

Fable Studio 146
Facebook 91–92, 112
false hero 61
Fazio, Patrik 14–15
fifty folk tales by computer 63–64
File Explorer 151
flashbacks 19, 59, 99
Fleming, Ian 21
Flores, Leo 43
folk tales 3, 57, 59, 61–64, 68
Ford, Harrison 104

Frayn, Michael 25
French, Scott 11, 53–54

generative networks 73–75
Generative Pre-trained Transformer
    (GPT) program 71
Gester 66–68
*Gestes et Opinions du Docteur Faustroll
    Pataphysicien: Roman Néo-scientifique
    Suivi de Spéculations* 35
"giant game of Consequences" 52
Godfather, The 22
gods of creation 142–143
Google 70–71
Gorky, Maxim 59
GPT-2 11, 70–71, 76
GPT-3 12, 76–79, 92, 103, 143, 147,
    150–151
Grand Theft Auto 87, 90
"Great Automatic Grammatizator, The" 24
Grimes, Joseph 62–63
Gulliver, Lemuel 23
Gulliver's Travels 23

Happy Spider story 79
harmony 2
Harry Potter books 60–61
helper 61
hero 21–22, 24, 60–63, 95, 106, 119, 133
hexameter mania 32–34
high focus thinking 116–117
homographic poems 38
Hughes, G. E. 52
human: behaviour 63; consciousness
    105; creativity 7, 13, 49, 112–114;
    imagination 13; language 18, 63;
    -quality blog posts 144; storytellers
    22; verbal interaction 18; writers 101;
    -written works 149
Humanoid Robotics Group at MIT 105
human story machines: creativity
    mechanized 23–25; epic tales 20–21;
    Internet heroes 22; learning by
    storytelling 15–17; living through
    stories 17–18; modern epics 21–22;
    power of story 19–20; storytelling,
    evolution of 18–19; wired for stories
    14–15

human storytelling, creativity
    in: combinatorial creativity
    102; conceptual creativity 106;
    experiential creativity 103–105
hunter-gatherer societies 19

Ihde, Don 118
immersive story-based games 147
Inception 22
indigenous nomadic communities 19
Institute of 'Pataphysics 39
intellectual and cultural sophistication
    58–59
interestingness 7, 124
internet: ConceptNet 112; data
    source 71; followers 22; heroes 22;
    influencers 22; storyworld 91
Iron Man movies 22
Ishiguro, Kazuo 149
Islanders 97

James Bond novels 21–22
Jarry, Alfred 35, 39
Jiejie, Furong 22
Joyce, James 52
Just This Once 11, 53–54, 145

kaleidoscopic evolution 33
Katz's Deli 22
Kazemi, Darius 55
King, Stephen 116, 118
Kipling, Rudyard 17
Klara and the Sun 149
Klein, Sheldon 2–3, 58, 63–65
Knipe, Adolph 24
knowledge-based generator of story
    outlines 147

Lakoff, George 64
language 147; evocative 87, 149;
    generation 143–145, 148–149;
    human 18, 63; neural network 12;
    rules and memory networks 48;
    structure 19
La Salle University 37
Latin verse machine 27–30
Lawrence, D. H. 52
Lego models 124

Levi-Strauss, Claude 61–62
life on internet, stories of 150–151
LIGHT (Learning in Interactive Games
  with Humans and Text) 91–92
lodging 56
low focus thinking 116–117

Macintosh, Charles 30
Manchester 39–40
Manchester University Computer 40
McCartney, Paul 39
Melpomene 52
memories and reassurance 141–142
mental scripts 17–18
mental time travel 18
meteorology models 124
MEXICA 116, 119–125, 147–148
mime acting 19
Minecraft 100
MINSTREL program 7–8, 26, 107–114,
  123–124
mis-spun tales 94
Montfort, Nick 43, 56, 99
Mori, Masahiro 81
Morley, David 101
Morphology of the Folktale 59–63, 106
Mueller, Erik T. 103, 105
murder flow-chart 3
music streaming 22
Musk, Elon 11, 22

NaNoGenMo 54–56
narrative computer games 90–91
"Narrative Structure in Fleming,
  The" 21
National Lampoon 3
National Novel Generation Month
  (NaNoGenMo) 54–56
Necklace, The 106
neural networks 68–69, 71–73, 103,
  112, 143, 150–151
New York Post 75
Nineteen Eighty-Four 11, 70

One Hundred Million Million Poems
  35–36
On Writing 116
OpenAI company 11–12, 76

Opoyaz 59
Orwell, George 11, 25, 70
Oulipo 34–36, 38–39, 41, 59, 102
"Ouvroir de Litterature Potentialle" 35

pataphysics 35
pay attention 78–79
Pemberton, Lyn 66
Pentametron 43–44
Perec, George 35
performers 146
personal blogs 147
personal companion 146, 150
Peter, John 27, 36
photorealistic graphics 145
Poland, Krakow 52
*Policeman's Beard Is Half Constructed,
  The* 10–11, 49–52
potential literature 36
Prelude, The 83
primary generator 116, 119
Propp, Vladimir 3, 59, 106
Publishers Weekly 54

Queneau, Raymond 35, 102

Racter 49–51, 56
randomness 23, 41, 102
rationalization 104–105
reader, imagination of 6–7
recovery 104–105
revenge 104–105
reversal 104–105
Revolt in Flatland 49
Robbins, Jerome 107
Roget's Thesaurus 24
romance fiction 10
Romeo and Juliet 107
roving 104–105
Rowling, J. K. 61
Russian fairy stories, and Harry Potter
  60–61
Ryan, James 97, 103

Saum, Alex 43
Schank, Roger 17–18
school education 16–17
Scientific American 11

Scott, Walter 24
self-affirming conformity 15
self-discipline 32
self-esteem 104–105
self-taught computer programmer 53
semantic memory 118
Sheldon County 99, 103, 151
Sherlock Holmes short stories 2
Shlovsky, Viktor Borisovich 58–59
Short Edition 1
short-term memory 117
sifting stories 96–99
Sir Cumference and the First Round Table 17
social behaviour 147
social distancing 18
social media 22, 43, 70, 143, 151
Sondheim, Stephen 107
Sony 145–146
Soviet realism 62
Space Invaders 145
Space Odyssey, A 113
speech and movement 14–15
Starynkevitch, Dimitri 41
stereotypical mystery story 2–3
story: grammars 4–5, 8, 64–68; outline 4–5; writing, engagement and reflection 119
storytellers 10, 20, 146
storytelling models 19, 22, 101, 147–150
story vending machines 1
storyworlds 143, 145–147; automating 91–92; characters 92–94; Colossal Cave Adventure 84–87; sifting stories 96–99; storytelling game, designing 87–91; tellable tales 94–96
Strachey, Christopher 40
Susann, Jacqueline 11, 54
Swift, Jonathan 24
Sybil of Cumae 23

Tales of the Crusadors 24
tellability 6–7
tellable tales 94–96, 151
text-based adventures 87
Tony Stark character 22
TRAMS 108, 113

Transform-Recall-Adapt Methods (TRAMS) 108
transportation 56
Turing, Alan 39
Twitter 43
Tyrolian minstrels 26
Tzara, Tristan 37

ultra-fast home gaming computers 145
untellable story 95
USA Today 75
Utnapishtim 20–21

Valley of the Dolls 145
Vantage Press 52
verbalization 19
villain 21, 60–63, 66, 106
virtual reality (VR) headset 146

Waterloo, Battle of 26
Watson computer program 103
Welsh dwarf 26
West Side Story 107
When Harry Met Sally 22
Wolves in the Walls 146
Wordsworth, William 83
Workshop of Potential Literature 35
World of Warcraft 100
writer mind 146; cognition and writing 115–116; creativity 112–113; Engagement-Reflection (E-R) writing model 115; focus thinking 116–117; knowledge as data structures 125; mental processes 115; MEXICA 119–123; model testing 123–125; and reader 44; rhythms 117–119
Writesonic 144
writing 36; automated story 49; creative 81, 150; models of 143

Yorke, Thom 38
your own story generator: headlines 126–129; Llull's generative truths 134–140; storyworld map 132–134; yoghurt pot stories 129–132

zombie-like characters 92–93

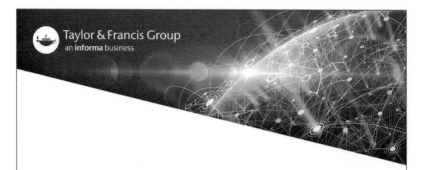